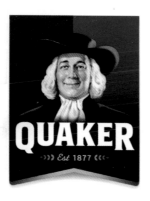

The
QUAKER OATS
Cookbook

 Real Possibilities

Romeo Langit
10603 Mackenzie Dr.
Houston, TX 77086

D1092634

Publications International, Ltd.

Quaker, the Quaker Man, Tropicana Pure Premium, Aunt Jemima, Oatmeal Squares, and Life—Trademarks of PepsiCo, Inc. and related companies. Used under license.

Pictured on the front cover *(clockwise from top):* Baked Cherry-Almond Oatmeal *(page 8)*, Asian Stuffed Mushrooms *(page 64)*, Fruit Crisp *(page 113)*, and Veggie Burgers *(page 46)*.
Pictured on the back cover: Double Orange Walnut Muffins *(page 24)*, Hearty Meatball Stew *(page 68)*, Saucy Stuffed Peppers *(page 45)*, and Chewy Oatmeal Spice Bars *(page 73)*.

ISBN: 978-1-4508-7782-4

Library of Congress Control Number: 2013945071

Manufactured in China.

8 7 6 5 4 3 2 1

Microwave Cooking: Microwave ovens vary in wattage. Use the cooking times as guidelines and check for doneness before adding more time.

Please visit **quakeroats.com** for more great recipes!

CONTENTS

Fun Twists to Traditional Oatmeal

Banana Bread Oatmeal

- 3 cups fat-free (skim) milk
- 3 tablespoons firmly packed brown sugar
- ¾ teaspoon ground cinnamon
- ¼ teaspoon ground nutmeg
- ¼ teaspoon salt (optional)
- 2 cups **QUAKER® Oats** (quick or old fashioned, uncooked)
- 1 cup mashed ripe bananas (about 3 medium)
- 2 tablespoons coarsely chopped toasted pecans
   Nonfat plain or vanilla yogurt (optional)
   Banana slices (optional)
   Pecan halves (optional)

1 Bring milk, brown sugar, cinnamon, nutmeg and salt, if desired, to a gentle boil in medium saucepan (watch carefully); stir in oats. Return to a boil; reduce heat to medium. Cook 1 minute for quick oats, 5 minutes for old fashioned oats, or until most of liquid is absorbed, stirring occasionally.

2 Remove oatmeal from heat. Stir in mashed bananas and chopped pecans. Spoon into six cereal bowls. Top with yogurt, sliced bananas and pecan halves, if desired.

Makes 6 servings

• Tip

To toast pecans, spread evenly in shallow baking pan. Bake at 350°F 5 to 7 minutes or until light golden brown, stirring occasionally. Cool before using. Or, spread nuts evenly on microwave-safe plate. Microwave on HIGH (100% power) 1 minute; stir. Continue to microwave on HIGH, checking every 30 seconds, until nuts are fragrant and brown. Cool before using.

Peach Cobbler Oatmeal

TOPPING

- ¼ cup toasted wheat germ
- 2 tablespoons firmly packed brown sugar
- ¼ teaspoon ground cinnamon

OATMEAL

- 3 cups fat-free (skim) milk
- 1 teaspoon ground cinnamon
- ½ teaspoon salt
- ⅛ to ¼ teaspoon ground nutmeg
- 2 cups **QUAKER® Oats** (quick or old fashioned, uncooked)
- 1¼ cups chopped frozen (thawed) or canned (drained) peaches
- 1 container (8 ounces) low-fat or fat-free vanilla yogurt

1 For topping, combine wheat germ, brown sugar and ¼ teaspoon cinnamon in small bowl. Set aside.

2 For oatmeal, bring milk, cinnamon, salt and nutmeg to a gentle boil in medium saucepan (watch carefully); stir in oats. Return to a boil; reduce heat to medium. Cook oats for 1 minute, stirring occasionally. Stir in peaches. Continue cooking, stirring occasionally, until peaches are heated through and most of liquid is absorbed, about 1 minute.

3 Spoon oatmeal into four cereal bowls. Top with wheat germ mixture and yogurt.

Makes 4 servings

Fun Twists to Traditional Oatmeal

Baked Cherry-Almond Oatmeal

2¼ cups **QUAKER® Oats** (quick or old fashioned, uncooked)

½ cup firmly packed brown sugar

½ teaspoon salt

3 cups reduced-fat (2%) milk

3 eggs, lightly beaten

1 tablespoon melted butter (optional)

1 teaspoon vanilla

¼ to ½ teaspoon almond extract

¾ cup dried cherries

½ cup toasted sliced almonds

Low-fat vanilla yogurt

1 Heat oven to 350°F. Spray 8 (6-ounce) custard cups or ramekins with nonstick cooking spray; arrange on rimmed baking sheet.

2 Combine oats, brown sugar and salt in large bowl; mix well. Whisk together milk, eggs, butter, if desired, vanilla and almond extract in medium bowl. Add to dry ingredients; mix until well blended. Spoon into cups. Stir cherries into each cup, dividing evenly; sprinkle evenly with almonds.

3 Bake until knife inserted near center comes out clean, about 23 to 26 minutes for quick oats, 25 to 30 minutes for old fashioned oats. (Centers will not be completely set.) Cool 10 minutes. To serve, top with yogurt.

Makes 8 servings

Variations:
Substitute dried cranberries, blueberries or chopped dried apricots for dried cherries.

To bake in 8-inch square baking pan, spray pan with nonstick cooking spray. Prepare oatmeal as directed. Pour into pan, stir in cherries and sprinkle with almonds. Bake until knife inserted near center comes out clean, about 30 to 35 minutes.

• Tip

To toast almonds, spread in single layer on cookie sheet. Bake at 350°F about 6 to 8 minutes or until lightly browned and fragrant, stirring occasionally. Cool before using. Or spread in single layer on microwave-safe plate. Microwave on HIGH (100% power) 1 minute; stir. Continue to microwave on HIGH, checking every 30 seconds, until nuts are fragrant and brown. Cool before using.

Fun Twists to Traditional Oatmeal

Creamy Maple Cranberry Oatmeal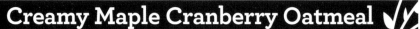

3½ cups fat-free (skim) or
    reduced-fat (2%) milk

2 cups **QUAKER® Oats** (quick or
    old fashioned, uncooked)

½ cup dried cranberries

⅓ cup **AUNT JEMIMA® Syrup,**
    regular or light

¼ cup toasted wheat germ
    Additional **AUNT JEMIMA®
    Syrup,** milk or yogurt
    (optional)

1 Bring milk to a gentle boil in medium saucepan (watch carefully). Stir in oats, cranberries and ⅓ cup syrup. Return to a boil; reduce heat to medium. Cook 1 minute for quick oats, 5 minutes for large flake oats, or until most of milk is absorbed, stirring occasionally. Let stand until desired consistency. Stir in wheat germ.

2 Spoon oatmeal into four cereal bowls. Drizzle with additional syrup, if desired. Serve with milk or yogurt, if desired.

Makes 4 servings

Microwave Directions: Combine all ingredients except wheat germ in 3-quart microwave-safe bowl. Microwave on HIGH (100% power) 6 to 7 minutes for quick oats, or until most of liquid is absorbed. Let stand until desired consistency. Stir in wheat germ.

•Tip

Freeze single servings of cooked oatmeal in small resealable freezer bags. Thaw in refrigerator overnight. Transfer to microwave-safe bowl. Microwave, covered, on DEFROST until hot, stirring once or twice.

Fun Twists to Traditional Oatmeal

Crunchy Muesli

1½ cups fat-free (skim) milk

1¼ cups **QUAKER® Oats** (quick or old fashioned, uncooked)

¼ cup raisins

¼ cup dried cranberries

¾ cup sweetened condensed milk

3 tablespoons lemon juice

1 medium Granny Smith apple, unpeeled, cut into thin strips

2 tablespoons slivered almonds

1 teaspoon nuts and seeds, chopped

Mint leaves (optional)

1 Combine milk, oats, raisins and cranberries in medium bowl; cover and refrigerate overnight.

2 Remove oat mixture from refrigerator; drain any excess liquid.

3 Add condensed milk, lemon juice, apple, almonds and nut/seed mixture; mix well. If desired, garnish with mint before serving.

Makes 2 to 3 servings

Orange Cranberry Oatmeal

2 cups **TROPICANA PURE PREMIUM® Orange Juice**
1 cup water
¼ teaspoon salt
⅛ teaspoon ground cinnamon
2 cups **QUAKER® Oats** (quick or old fashioned, uncooked)

½ cup dried cranberries
1 cup low-fat or fat-free vanilla yogurt
¼ cup chopped toasted walnuts
Additional dried cranberries (optional)

1 Bring orange juice, water, salt and cinnamon to a gentle boil in medium saucepan. Stir in oats and cranberries. Return to a boil; reduce heat to medium. Cook 1 minute for quick oats, 5 minutes for old fashioned oats, or until most of liquid is absorbed, stirring occasionally. Let stand until desired consistency.

2 Spoon oatmeal into four cereal bowls. Top each serving with ¼ cup yogurt, 1 tablespoon walnuts and additional cranberries, if desired.

Makes 4 servings

Microwave Directions: Combine all ingredients except yogurt and nuts in 3-quart microwaveable bowl. Microwave on HIGH (100% power) 4 to 6 minutes for quick oats, 7 to 9 minutes for old fashioned oats, or until most of the liquid is absorbed. Let stand until desired consistency. Top each serving with yogurt, walnuts and additional cranberries, if desired.

• Tip

To toast walnuts, spread in single layer in heavy-bottomed skillet. Cook over medium heat 1 to 2 minutes, stirring frequently, until nuts are lightly browned. Remove from skillet immediately. Cool before using.

Fun Twists to Traditional Oatmeal

Basil Berry and Walnut Oatmeal

BERRY GASTRIQUE

- ¼ shallot, peeled and minced
- 1 teaspoon unsalted butter
- 2 cups fresh berries (strawberries, raspberries, blueberries)
- 4 to 5 tablespoons granulated sugar (depending on the sweetness of the berries)
- 3 tablespoons white wine
- 2 teaspoons white wine vinegar
  Pinch of salt

OATMEAL

- 1 cup **QUAKER® Kettle Hearty Oats**
- 1¾ cups water
- ⅛ cup orange juice
- 2 teaspoons granulated sugar

- 1 cup fresh berries for garnish
- ½ cup walnuts, chopped and toasted
  Fresh basil, chiffonade

1 For gastrique, cook shallot in butter over medium-low heat in large saucepan until translucent, about 5 minutes.

2 Add berries, sugar, white wine, vinegar and salt. Bring to a boil; reduce to a simmer and cook until fruit is very tender, about 15 minutes.

3 Purée mixture in blender or with immersion blender; then pass through a fine mesh strainer to remove fine seeds.

4 Taste to adjust seasonings and tartness. Chill until ready to serve.

ASSEMBLY

5 For oatmeal, bring oats, water, orange juice and 2 teaspoons sugar to gentle boil in medium saucepan. Continue cooking until water is absorbed.

6 Serve each portion of oatmeal with drizzle of the berry gastrique. Garnish with fresh berries, walnuts and basil.

Makes approximately 4 servings

Fun Twists to Traditional Oatmeal

Apricot Honey Oatmeal

3½ cups water
 ⅓ cup chopped dried apricots
 ¼ cup honey
 ½ teaspoon ground cinnamon
 2 cups **QUAKER® Oats** (quick or old fashioned, uncooked)

Bring water, apricots, honey and cinnamon to a boil in 3-quart saucepan; stir in oats. Return to a boil; reduce heat to medium. Cook 1 minute for quick oats, 5 minutes for old fashioned oats, or until most of liquid is absorbed, stirring occasionally. Let stand until desired consistency.

Makes 4 servings

• Tip

If desired, substitute raisins, dried peaches or pears, dried cranberries or blueberries, dried apples, dates or diced mixed dried fruit for the apricots.

Pineapple-Macadamia Oatmeal

1 can (20 ounces) pineapple tidbits in pineapple juice	2 containers (6 ounces each) fat-free vanilla yogurt*
Water	¼ to ½ teaspoon ground ginger
¼ teaspoon salt	⅓ cup packed brown sugar*
2 cups **QUAKER® Oats** (quick or old fashioned, uncooked)	¼ cup coarsely chopped macadamia nuts or almonds

If artificially sweetened yogurt is used, reduce brown sugar to ¼ cup.

1 Drain pineapple tidbits, reserving juice. Set fruit aside. Add enough water to juice to equal 3¼ cups. Bring combined juice and water and salt to a boil in medium saucepan. Stir in oats.

2 Return to a boil; reduce heat to medium. Cook 1 minute for quick oats, 5 minutes for old fashioned oats, or until most of liquid is absorbed, stirring occasionally. Stir in reserved pineapple. Let stand, covered, until desired consistency.

3 Spoon yogurt into small bowl. Add ginger; mix well. Spoon oatmeal into five cereal bowls. Top each serving with brown sugar, nuts and yogurt, dividing evenly.

Makes 5 servings

Fruit and Honey Granola

3½ cups **QUAKER® Oats** (quick or old fashioned, uncooked)

2 tablespoons coarsely chopped pecans

½ cup honey

2 tablespoons vegetable oil

1 teaspoon vanilla

½ teaspoon ground cinnamon

⅛ to ¼ teaspoon salt (optional)

1 package (6 ounces) diced dried mixed fruit (about 1⅓ cups)

1 Heat oven to 350°F.

2 Combine oats and pecans in large bowl; mix well. Spread evenly in 15×10-inch jelly-roll pan or on rimmed baking sheet. Combine honey, oil, vanilla, cinnamon and salt, if desired, in small bowl; mix well. Pour over oat mixture; mix well.

3 Bake 30 to 35 minutes or until golden brown, stirring every 10 minutes. Cool completely in pan. Stir in dried fruit. Store in tightly-covered container for up to one week.

Makes 11 servings

Variation: Substitute dried cranberries, chopped dried apricots or chopped dried peaches for dried mixed fruit.

Baked Oatmeal Brûlée

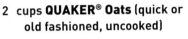

2 cups **QUAKER® Oats** (quick or old fashioned, uncooked)

⅓ cup granulated sugar

3⅓ cups fat-free (skim) milk

½ cup liquid egg substitute with yolk or 2 eggs, lightly beaten

2 teaspoons vanilla

⅓ cup firmly packed brown sugar

1 Heat oven to 350°F. Spray 8-inch square glass baking dish with nonstick cooking spray.

2 Combine oats and granulated sugar in large bowl. Combine milk, egg substitute and vanilla in medium bowl; mix well. Add to oat mixture; mix well. Pour into baking dish.

3 Bake 40 to 45 minutes or until center jiggles slightly. Remove from oven to wire rack.

4 Sprinkle brown sugar evenly over top of oatmeal. Using back of spoon, gently spread into thin layer across entire surface of oatmeal. Return to oven; bake just until sugar melts, about 2 to 3 minutes. Set oven to broil. Broil 3 inches from heat until sugar bubbles and browns slightly, 1 to 2 minutes. (Watch carefully to prevent burning. It may be necessary to turn baking dish.) Spoon into bowls to serve.

Makes 8 servings

Berry Almond Crumble Oatmeal

TOPPING

- ½ cup **QUAKER® Oats** (quick or old fashioned, uncooked)
- ¼ cup sliced almonds
- ⅓ cup firmly packed brown sugar
- ½ teaspoon ground cinnamon

OATMEAL

- 3 cups fat-free (skim) milk or low-fat soy drink
- 1½ teaspoons ground cinnamon
- 2 cups **QUAKER® Oats** (quick or old fashioned, uncooked)
- 1 cup blueberries, frozen (do not thaw) or canned (drained)

1 For topping, combine oats and almonds in medium skillet. Cook over medium-low heat 4 to 6 minutes, stirring occasionally, until both are lightly browned. Cool completely. Combine brown sugar and cinnamon in small bowl. Add oat mixture; mix well. Set aside.

2 For oatmeal, bring milk and cinnamon to a boil in medium saucepan; stir in oats. Return to a boil; reduce heat to medium. Cook 1 minute for quick oats, 5 minutes for old fashioned oats, stirring occasionally. Gently stir in blueberries. Continue cooking, until blueberries are heated through and most of liquid is absorbed, about 1 minute.

3 Spoon oatmeal into five cereal bowls. Sprinkle topping over oatmeal.

Makes 5 servings

• Tips

To toast oats and almonds in a microwave oven, combine oats and almonds in a glass pie plate. Heat on HIGH (100% power) 2 to 4 minutes or until light golden brown, stirring every minute. Cool completely. Proceed as directed.

To toast oats and almonds in the oven, heat oven to 350°F. Place oats in a shallow baking pan. Bake 5 minutes, stirring once. Add almonds and continue baking 5 minutes, stirring occasionally, until oats and almonds are golden brown. Cool completely. Proceed as directed.

Wake Up
to Muffins
& Quick Breads

Oatmeal Herb Bread

2½   teaspoons quick-rising yeast

2¾   cups bread flour

1   cup **QUAKER®** Oats (quick or old fashioned, uncooked)

½   cup grated Parmesan cheese

1   tablespoon granulated sugar

1   teaspoon salt

½   teaspoon Italian seasoning blend or dried dill weed

1⅓   cups buttermilk

2   tablespoons vegetable oil (preferably olive oil)

1 Bring all refrigerated ingredients to room temperature by letting them stand on counter about 30 minutes.

2 Place yeast in bread machine pan according to directions in manual. Combine flour, oats, cheese, sugar, salt and Italian seasoning in medium bowl; mix well. Combine buttermilk and oil in separate bowl; mix well.

3 Place dry ingredients and buttermilk mixture in bread machine pan according to manual. Select white bread and light crust settings. Remove bread from pan to wire rack. Cool completely before slicing.

Makes 1 loaf (16 servings)

• Tip

Refrigerated ingredients (except eggs) can be warmed to room temperature quickly by microwaving them for 15 to 20 seconds on HIGH (100% power).

Double Orange Walnut Muffins

1½ cups all-purpose flour*

1 cup **QUAKER® Oats** (quick or old fashioned, uncooked)

⅔ cup plus 1 tablespoon granulated sugar, divided

2 teaspoons baking powder

½ teaspoon baking soda

¼ teaspoon salt

¾ cup coarsely chopped toasted walnuts,** divided

⅔ cup plus ¼ cup **TROPICANA PURE PREMIUM® Orange Juice**, divided

½ cup low-fat (1%) or fat-free (skim) milk

1 large egg

¼ cup (½ stick) butter or margarine, melted and cooled

If using old fashioned oats, add 2 tablespoons additional flour.

**To toast walnuts, spread in single layer in heavy-bottomed skillet. Cook over medium heat 1 to 2 minutes, stirring frequently, until nuts are lightly browned. Remove from skillet immediately. Cool before using.*

1 Heat oven to 400°F. Line 12 medium muffin cups with paper baking cups or spray bottoms only with nonstick cooking spray.

2 Stir together flour, oats, ⅔ cup sugar, baking powder, baking soda and salt in large bowl. Add ½ cup walnuts; mix well. Set aside. Beat ⅔ cup juice, milk, egg and butter with whisk or fork in medium bowl until well blended. Add to dry ingredients all at once; stir just until dry ingredients are moistened. (Do not overmix.)

3 Pour into muffin cups, dividing evenly. Sprinkle tops with remaining ¼ cup walnuts.

4 Bake 15 to 18 minutes or until wooden pick inserted in centers comes out clean. Remove pan from oven and immediately spoon remaining ¼ cup orange juice over muffin tops, dividing evenly. Let stand 5 minutes. Sprinkle muffin tops with remaining 1 tablespoon sugar. Remove from pan. Serve warm.

Makes 12 muffins

•Tip

Chopped toasted pecans may be substituted for walnuts.

Nuts may be omitted, if desired.

Oaty Pear 'n' Pecan Pancakes

1 cup **AUNT JEMIMA® Original Pancake Mix**

1 teaspoon ground cinnamon

1 cup milk

1 egg

1 tablespoon vegetable oil

1 medium-firm ripe pear, cored and chopped (about 1 cup)

¾ cup **QUAKER® Oats** (quick or old fashioned, uncooked)

2 tablespoons chopped toasted pecans

½ to ¾ cup **AUNT JEMIMA LITE® Syrup**, warmed

Pear slices (optional)

Chopped toasted pecans (optional)

1 Stir together pancake mix and cinnamon in large bowl. Combine milk, egg and oil in medium bowl; mix well. Add to pancake mix; stir with wire whisk just until combined. Gently stir in chopped pear, oats and 2 tablespoons pecans. Let stand 1 to 2 minutes to thicken.

2 Cook pancakes on hot griddle according to package directions. Serve with syrup and, if desired, pear slices and additional pecans.

Makes 12 pancakes

• Tip

To toast pecans, spread in single layer on cookie sheet. Bake at 350°F about 6 to 8 minutes or until lightly browned and fragrant, stirring occasionally. Cool before using. Or spread in single layer on microwave-safe plate. Microwave on HIGH (100% power) 1 minute; stir. Continue to microwave on HIGH, checking every 30 seconds, until nuts are fragrant and brown. Cool before using.

Wake Up to Muffins & Quick Breads

Cinnamon Bun Scones

2 cups all-purpose flour

1 cup **QUAKER® Oats** (quick or old fashioned, uncooked)

¼ cup plus 2 tablespoons granulated sugar, divided

1 tablespoon baking powder

¼ teaspoon salt

½ cup (1 stick) butter, chilled and cut into pieces

¾ cup whole or reduced-fat (2%) milk

1 egg, lightly beaten

1 teaspoon vanilla

½ cup toasted chopped pecans

2 teaspoons ground cinnamon

¾ cup powdered sugar

3 to 4 teaspoons **TROPICANA PURE PREMIUM® Orange Juice** or milk

1 Heat oven to 425°F. Spray cookie sheet with nonstick cooking spray.

2 Combine flour, oats, ¼ cup granulated sugar, baking powder and salt in large bowl; mix well. Cut in butter with pastry blender or two knives until mixture resembles coarse crumbs. Combine milk, egg and vanilla in small bowl; blend well. Add to dry ingredients all at once; stir with fork or rubber spatula until dry ingredients are moistened.

3 Combine remaining 2 tablespoons granulated sugar with pecans and cinnamon in small bowl; mix well. Sprinkle evenly over dough in bowl; gently stir batter to swirl in cinnamon mixture. (Do not blend completely.) Drop dough by ¼ cupfuls 2 inches apart on cookie sheet.

4 Bake 11 to 13 minutes or until golden brown. Remove to wire rack; cool 5 minutes. In small bowl, combine powdered sugar and enough orange juice for desired consistency; mix until smooth. Drizzle over top of warm scones. Serve warm.

Makes 12 scones

Caramel-Nut Sticky Biscuits

TOPPING

⅔ cup firmly packed brown sugar

¼ cup light corn syrup

¼ cup (½ stick) margarine, melted

½ teaspoon ground cinnamon

1 cup pecan halves

BISCUITS

2 cups all-purpose flour

1 cup **QUAKER®
Oats** (quick or old fashioned, uncooked)

¼ cup granulated sugar

1 tablespoon baking powder

¾ teaspoon baking soda

½ teaspoon salt (optional)

½ teaspoon ground cinnamon

⅓ cup (5⅓ tablespoons) margarine

1 cup buttermilk*

*Sour milk can be substituted for buttermilk. For 1 cup sour milk, combine 1 tablespoon vinegar or lemon juice and enough milk to make 1 cup; let stand 5 minutes.

1 Heat oven to 425°F. For topping, combine first four ingredients; mix well. Spread onto bottom of 9-inch square baking pan. Sprinkle with pecans; set aside.

2 For biscuits, combine dry ingredients; mix well. Cut in margarine with pastry blender or two knives until crumbly. Stir in buttermilk, mixing just until moistened. Knead gently on lightly floured surface 5 to 7 times; pat into 8-inch square. Cut with knife into 16 (2-inch) square biscuits; place over topping in pan. Bake 25 to 28 minutes or until golden brown. Let stand 3 minutes; invert onto large platter. Serve warm.

Makes 16 servings

Applesauce Oatmeal Muffins

TOPPING

- ¼ cup **QUAKER®** Oats (quick or old fashioned, uncooked)
- 1 tablespoon firmly packed brown sugar
- 1 tablespoon light butter or butter, melted
- ¼ teaspoon ground cinnamon

MUFFINS

- 1½ cups **QUAKER®** Oats (quick or old fashioned, uncooked)
- 1¼ cups all-purpose flour
- 1 teaspoon baking powder
- ¾ teaspoon baking soda
- ¾ teaspoon ground cinnamon
- 1 cup unsweetened applesauce
- ½ cup fat-free (skim) milk
- ⅓ cup firmly packed brown sugar
- 3 tablespoons canola oil
- ¼ cup liquid egg substitute with yolk or 1 egg, lightly beaten

1 Heat oven to 400°F. Line 12 medium muffin cups with paper baking cups or spray bottoms only with nonstick cooking spray. For topping, combine ¼ cup oats, 1 tablespoon brown sugar, butter and cinnamon in small bowl; mix well. Set aside.

2 For muffins, combine 1½ cups oats, flour, baking powder, baking soda and cinnamon in large bowl; mix well. Combine applesauce, milk, ⅓ cup brown sugar, oil and egg substitute in medium bowl; blend well. Add to dry ingredients all at once; stir just until dry ingredients are moistened. (Do not overmix.)

3 Fill muffin cups almost full. Sprinkle with reserved topping, patting gently.

4 Bake 20 to 22 minutes or until golden brown. Cool muffins in pan on wire rack 5 minutes. Remove from pan. Serve warm.

Makes 12 muffins

Italian Herbed Oatmeal Focaccia

2 tablespoons cornmeal

1½ to 2¼ cups all-purpose flour

1 cup **QUAKER® Oats** (quick or old fashioned, uncooked)

2 tablespoons Italian seasoning blend, divided

1 package (¼ ounce) quick-rising yeast (about 2¼ teaspoons)

2 teaspoons granulated sugar

1½ teaspoons garlic salt, divided

1 cup water

¼ cup plus 2 tablespoons olive oil, divided

4 to 6 sun-dried tomatoes packed in oil, drained and chopped

¼ cup shredded Parmesan cheese

1 Lightly spray 13×9-inch baking pan with nonstick cooking spray; dust with cornmeal.

2 Combine 1 cup flour, oats, 1 tablespoon Italian seasoning, yeast, sugar and 1 teaspoon garlic salt in large bowl; mix well. Heat water and ¼ cup oil in small saucepan until very warm (120°F to 130°F). Add to flour mixture; mix well. Gradually stir in enough remaining flour to make a soft dough.

3 Turn dough out onto lightly floured surface. Knead 8 to 10 minutes or until smooth and elastic. Cover; let rest 10 minutes.

4 Pat dough into prepared pan, pressing dough out to edges of pan. Using fingertips, poke indentations over surface of dough. Brush dough with remaining 2 tablespoons oil. Sprinkle with remaining 1 tablespoon Italian seasoning and ½ teaspoon garlic salt. Arrange sun-dried tomatoes across top; sprinkle with cheese. Cover; let rise in warm place 30 minutes or until doubled in size.

5 Heat oven to 400°F. Bake 25 to 30 minutes or until golden brown. Cut into strips or squares. Serve warm.

Makes 12 servings

Oatmeal Carrot Cake Bread

1 cup **QUAKER® Oats** (quick or old fashioned, uncooked)

½ cup fat-free (skim) milk

1 can (8 ounces) crushed pineapple in juice, undrained

2 large eggs, lightly beaten

¼ cup vegetable oil

1 teaspoon vanilla

1½ cups all-purpose flour

1 cup whole-wheat flour

1 cup firmly packed brown sugar

1 tablespoon baking powder

½ teaspoon baking soda

½ teaspoon ground cinnamon

¼ teaspoon salt

1½ cups shredded carrots (about 3 medium)

½ cup raisins

½ cup chopped walnuts

1 Heat oven to 350°F. Lightly grease or spray bottom only of two 8×4-inch loaf pans or one 9×5-inch loaf pan with nonstick cooking spray.

2 Combine oats and milk in medium bowl; mix well. Let stand 10 minutes. Add pineapple (including juice), eggs, oil and vanilla; mix well.

3 Combine all-purpose flour, whole-wheat flour, brown sugar, baking powder, baking soda, cinnamon and salt in large bowl; mix well. Stir in carrots, raisins and walnuts. Add oat mixture to dry ingredients all at once; stir just until dry ingredients are moistened. (Do not overmix.) Pour batter into prepared pans.

4 Bake 45 to 55 minutes for 8×4-inch pans, or 60 to 75 minutes for 9×5-inch pan or until wooden pick inserted in center comes out clean and crust is golden brown. Cool in pan on wire rack 10 minutes. Remove from pan. Cool completely. Store tightly wrapped.

Makes 16 servings

Wake Up to Muffins & Quick Breads

Banana-Nana Pecan Bread

1 cup **QUAKER® Oats** (quick or old fashioned, uncooked)

½ cup chopped pecans

3 tablespoons margarine or butter, melted

2 tablespoons firmly packed brown sugar

1 package (14 ounces) banana bread quick bread mix

1 cup water

½ cup mashed ripe banana (about 1 large)

2 eggs, lightly beaten

3 tablespoons canola oil

1 Heat oven to 375°F. Grease and flour bottom only of 9×5-inch loaf pan.

2 Combine oats, pecans, margarine and brown sugar in small bowl; mix well. Reserve ½ cup mixture; set aside. Combine remaining oat mixture, quick bread mix, water, banana, eggs and oil in large bowl. Mix just until dry ingredients are moistened. Pour into prepared pan. Sprinkle top of loaf with reserved oat mixture.

3 Bake 50 to 55 minutes or until wooden pick inserted in center of loaf comes out clean. Cool 10 minutes in pan; remove to wire rack. Cool completely.

Makes 12 servings

Lemon Blueberry Oatmeal Muffins

TOPPING

- ¼ cup **QUAKER® Oats** (quick or old fashioned, uncooked)
- 2 tablespoons firmly packed brown sugar

MUFFINS

- 1½ cups **QUAKER® Oats** (quick or old fashioned, uncooked)
- 1 cup all-purpose flour*
- ½ cup granulated sugar
- 1 tablespoon baking powder
- ¼ teaspoon salt (optional)
- 1 cup fat-free (skim) milk
- 2 egg whites or ¼ cup egg substitute with yolk or 1 egg
- 2 tablespoons canola oil
- 1 teaspoon grated lemon peel
- 1 teaspoon vanilla
- 1 cup fresh or frozen blueberries (do not thaw)

*If using old fashioned oats, add 2 tablespoons additional flour.

1 Heat oven to 400°F. Spray 12 medium muffin cups with nonstick cooking spray. For topping, combine oats and brown sugar in small bowl. Set aside.

2 For muffins, combine oats, flour, granulated sugar, baking powder and salt, if desired, in large bowl; mix well. Combine milk, egg whites, oil, lemon peel and vanilla in small bowl; mix well. Add to dry ingredients all at once; stir just until dry ingredients are moistened. (Do not overmix.) Gently stir in berries. Fill muffin cups almost full; sprinkle with topping.

3 Bake 18 to 22 minutes or until light golden brown. Cool muffins in pan on wire rack 5 minutes. Remove from pan. Serve warm.

Makes 12 muffins

Apricot-Banana-Almond Bread

2½ cups all-purpose flour, plus flour for dusting pan

1 cup **QUAKER® Oats** (quick or old fashioned, uncooked)

2 teaspoons baking powder

1 teaspoon baking soda

½ teaspoon salt

⅔ cup finely chopped dried apricots

¼ cup plus 2 tablespoons unblanched sliced almonds, divided

1 cup mashed ripe bananas (about 2 medium bananas)

½ cup low-fat buttermilk

⅓ cup vegetable oil

⅓ cup packed light brown sugar

2 eggs

¼ teaspoon almond extract

1 Heat oven to 350°F. Spray bottom only of 9×5-inch loaf pan with nonstick cooking spray. Coat bottom of pan with flour; tap out excess.

2 Combine flour, oats, baking powder, baking soda and salt in large bowl; mix well. Add apricots and ¼ cup almonds; mix well.

3 Whisk together bananas, buttermilk, oil, brown sugar, eggs and almond extract in medium bowl until well blended. Add to dry ingredients all at once; stir just until dry ingredients are evenly moistened. (Do not overmix.) Pour into pan. Sprinkle with remaining 2 tablespoons almonds.

4 Bake 55 to 65 minutes or until golden brown and wooden pick inserted in center comes out clean. Cool 10 minutes in pan on wire rack. Remove bread from pan. Cool completely on rack.

Makes 1 loaf

Note: To store, wrap covered bread tightly in aluminum foil and store up to 3 days at room temperature. For longer storage, label and freeze.

Multi-Grain Apricot Oat Muffins

1 cup **QUAKER® Oats** (quick or old fashioned, uncooked)

1 cup whole-wheat flour*

½ cup firmly packed brown sugar

⅓ cup toasted wheat germ

2 teaspoons baking powder

1½ teaspoons grated orange peel

1 teaspoon ground cinnamon

½ teaspoon salt

1 cup fat-free (skim) milk

2 egg whites, lightly beaten

¼ cup vegetable oil

¼ cup apricot fruit spread, plus additional for glaze

Additional oats, for topping

*If using old fashioned oats, add 2 tablespoons additional flour.

1 Heat oven to 400°F. Line 12 medium muffin cups with paper baking cups. Set aside.

2 Combine oats, flour, brown sugar, wheat germ, baking powder, orange peel, cinnamon and salt in large bowl; mix well. Combine milk, egg whites and oil; mix well. Add to dry ingredients all at once; stir just until blended. (Batter will be thin.)

3 Fill muffin cups ⅓ full with batter. Carefully spoon 1 teaspoon apricot fruit spread into center of each muffin cup. Spoon remaining batter over fruit spread, dividing evenly. Sprinkle each filled muffin cup with additional oats.

4 Bake 20 to 22 minutes or until golden brown. Remove from oven to wire rack. Lightly brush additional fruit spread onto warm muffin tops to glaze. Let stand 10 minutes. Remove from pan. Serve warm.

Makes 12 muffins

•Tip

To freeze, wrap cooled muffins securely in foil, or place in freezer bag. Seal, label and freeze up to 6 months.

Wake Up to Muffins & Quick Breads

Fruit and Oat Scones

1½ cups all-purpose flour

1 cup **QUAKER® Oats** (quick or old fashioned, uncooked)

Heat-stable sugar substitute equal to 3 tablespoons granulated sugar

1½ teaspoons baking powder

½ teaspoon baking soda

½ teaspoon ground cinnamon

¼ teaspoon salt (optional)

5 tablespoons margarine, chilled and cut into pieces

⅓ cup finely chopped dried mixed fruit, dried cranberries or raisins

⅔ cup low-fat buttermilk

¼ cup egg substitute or 2 egg whites, lightly beaten

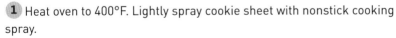

1 Heat oven to 400°F. Lightly spray cookie sheet with nonstick cooking spray.

2 Combine flour, oats, sugar substitute, baking powder, baking soda, cinnamon and salt, if desired, in large bowl; mix well. Cut in margarine with pastry blender or two knives until mixture resembles coarse crumbs. Stir in dried fruit. Add combined buttermilk and egg substitute to dry ingredients all at once; stir with fork just until dry ingredients are moistened. (Do not overmix.)

3 Drop dough by ¼ cup portions 2 inches apart onto cookie sheet. Bake 12 to 15 minutes or until very light golden brown. Serve warm.

Makes 10 scones

Tangy Buttermilk Cheese Bread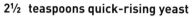

2½ teaspoons quick-rising yeast	1½ teaspoons salt
2¾ cups bread flour	¾ cup (3 ounces) shredded sharp Cheddar cheese
1 cup **QUAKER® Oats** (quick or old fashioned, uncooked)	1⅓ cups buttermilk
2 tablespoons granulated sugar	

1 Bring all refrigerated ingredients to room temperature by letting them stand on counter about 30 minutes.

2 Place yeast in bread machine pan according to directions in manual. Combine flour, oats, sugar and salt in medium bowl; mix well. Stir in cheese.

3 Place dry ingredients and buttermilk in bread machine pan according to manual. Select white bread and light crust settings. Remove bread from pan to wire rack. Cool completely before slicing.

Makes 1 loaf (16 servings)

• Tip

Refrigerated ingredients (except eggs) can be warmed to room temperature quickly by microwaving them for 15 to 20 seconds on HIGH (100% power).

Cinnamon Oat Rolls

1 pound frozen bread dough, thawed according to package directions

1 cup **QUAKER® Oats** (quick or old fashioned, uncooked)

⅓ cup firmly packed brown sugar

2 teaspoons ground cinnamon

⅓ cup (5 tablespoons plus 1 teaspoon) margarine or butter, melted

¾ cup raisins or dried cranberries

¼ cup orange marmalade

1 Let dough stand, covered, at room temperature 15 minutes to relax. Spray 8- or 9-inch square baking pan with nonstick cooking spray.

2 Combine oats, brown sugar and cinnamon in medium bowl. Add margarine; mix well. Stir in raisins. Set aside.

3 Roll dough into 12×10-inch rectangle. (Dough will be very elastic.) Spread evenly with oat mixture to within ½ inch of edges. Starting from long side, roll up; pinch seam to seal. With sharp knife, cut into 9 slices about 1¼ inches wide; place in prepared pan, cut sides down. Cover loosely with plastic wrap; let rise in warm place 30 minutes or until nearly doubled in size.

4 Heat oven to 350°F. Bake 30 to 35 minutes or until golden brown. Cool 5 minutes in pan on wire rack; remove from pan. Spread tops of rolls with marmalade. Serve warm.

Makes 9 rolls

Hearty Banana Oat Flapjacks

2 large ripe bananas, peeled and sliced

1 tablespoon granulated sugar

1 cup all-purpose flour

½ cup **QUAKER® Oats** (quick or old fashioned, uncooked)

1 tablespoon baking powder

¼ teaspoon ground cinnamon

¼ teaspoon salt (optional)

1 cup fat-free (skim) milk

1 egg, lightly beaten

2 tablespoons vegetable oil

AUNT JEMIMA® Syrup, warmed

Additional banana slices (optional)

Coarsely chopped pecans or walnuts (optional)

1 Combine banana slices and sugar in medium bowl; stir to coat slices with sugar. Set aside.

2 Combine flour, oats, baking powder, cinnamon and salt, if desired, in large bowl; mix well. Combine milk, egg and oil in medium bowl; blend well. Add to dry ingredients all at once; stir just until dry ingredients are moistened. (Do not overmix.)

3 Heat griddle over medium-high heat (or preheat electric skillet or griddle to 375°F). Lightly grease griddle. For each pancake, pour scant ¼ cup batter onto hot griddle. Top with four or five sugar-coated banana slices. Turn pancakes when tops are covered with bubbles and edges look cooked.

4 Serve with warm syrup and additional banana slices and nuts, if desired.

Makes 12 (4-inch) pancakes

Smart Lunch & Dinner Dishes

Saucy Stuffed Peppers

6 medium green bell peppers
1¼ cups water
2 cups low-sodium tomato juice, divided
1 can (6 ounces) tomato paste
1 teaspoon dried oregano leaves, divided
½ teaspoon dried basil leaves
½ teaspoon garlic powder, divided
1 pound lean ground beef
1½ cups **QUAKER® Oats** (quick or old fashioned, uncooked)
1 medium tomato, chopped
¼ cup chopped carrot
¼ cup chopped onion

1 Heat oven to 350°F. Cut bell peppers lengthwise in half; remove membranes and seeds. Set aside.

2 For sauce, combine water, 1 cup tomato juice, tomato paste, ½ teaspoon oregano, basil and ¼ teaspoon garlic powder in medium saucepan over medium heat. Simmer 10 to 15 minutes. Set aside.

3 For filling, combine beef, oats, tomato, carrot and onion with remaining 1 cup tomato juice, remaining ½ teaspoon oregano and ¼ teaspoon garlic powder in large bowl, mixing lightly but thoroughly.

4 Fill each bell pepper half with about ⅓ cup meat mixture. Place in 13×9-inch glass baking dish; pour reserved sauce evenly over bell peppers. Bake 45 to 50 minutes to medium doneness or until thermometer inserted into center of meat registers 160°F and juices show no pink color.

Makes 12 servings

Veggie Burgers

3 teaspoons vegetable oil, divided

1 cup sliced mushrooms

1 cup shredded carrots (about 2)

¾ cup chopped onion (about 1 medium)

¾ cup chopped zucchini (about 1 small)

2 cups **QUAKER® Oats** (quick or old fashioned, uncooked)

1 can (15 ounces) kidney beans, rinsed and drained

1 cup cooked white or brown rice

2 tablespoons soy sauce or ½ teaspoon salt

1 teaspoon minced garlic

⅛ teaspoon black pepper

½ cup chopped fresh cilantro or chives (optional)

Hamburger buns and toppings (optional)

1 Heat 1 teaspoon oil in large nonstick skillet. Add mushrooms, carrots, onion and zucchini; cook over medium-high heat 5 minutes or until vegetables are tender.

2 Transfer vegetables to food processor bowl. Add oats, beans, rice, soy sauce, garlic, pepper and cilantro, if desired. Pulse about 20 seconds or until well blended. Divide into 8 (½-cup) portions. Shape into patties between waxed paper. Refrigerate at least 1 hour or until firm.

3 Heat remaining 2 teaspoons oil in same skillet over medium-high heat. Cook patties 3 to 4 minutes on each side or until golden brown. Serve on buns with toppings, if desired.

Makes 8 servings

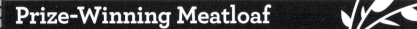

Prize-Winning Meatloaf

1½ pounds 90% lean ground beef	1 egg or 2 egg whites, lightly beaten
1 cup tomato juice or tomato sauce	¼ cup chopped onion
¾ cup **QUAKER® Oats** (quick or old fashioned, uncooked)	½ teaspoon salt (optional)
	¼ teaspoon black pepper

1 Heat oven to 350°F. Combine beef, tomato juice, oats, egg, onion, salt, if desired, and pepper in large bowl, mixing lightly but thoroughly. Shape into 8×4-inch loaf on rack in broiler pan.

2 Bake 1 hour to medium doneness (160°F) until no longer pink in center and juices show no pink color. Let stand 5 minutes.

Makes 8 servings

Serving Suggestion: Customize meatloaf by adding one of the following: ½ cup frozen (thawed) or canned (drained) corn; ½ cup chopped green or red bell pepper; 1 jar (2½ ounces) sliced mushrooms, drained; ⅓ cup grated Parmesan cheese; 2 tablespoons finely chopped fresh parsley or cilantro.

Tips

Sprinkle top of baked meatloaf with 1 cup shredded cheese. Return to oven for 3 minutes to melt cheese.

Spoon heated prepared spaghetti sauce, pizza sauce, barbecue sauce or salsa over each serving.

Smart Lunch & Dinner Dishes

Dilled Salmon Cakes

SAUCE

- ½ cup fat-free plain yogurt
- ⅓ cup seeded chopped tomato
- ⅓ cup seeded chopped cucumber
- 1 tablespoon finely chopped onion
- 1 tablespoon finely chopped fresh dill or 1 teaspoon dried dill weed

SALMON CAKES

- 1 can (14¾ ounces) pink salmon, drained, skin and bones removed
- ¾ cup **QUAKER® Oats** (quick or old fashioned, uncooked)
- ⅓ cup fat-free (skim) milk
- ¼ cup liquid egg substitute with yolk or 1 egg, lightly beaten
- 2 tablespoons finely chopped onion
- 1 tablespoon finely chopped fresh dill or 1 teaspoon dried dill weed
- ¼ teaspoon salt (optional)

1 For sauce, combine yogurt, tomato, cucumber, onion and dill in small bowl; mix well. Cover and chill.

2 For salmon cakes, combine salmon, oats, milk, egg substitute, onion, dill and salt, if desired, in medium bowl; mix well. Let stand 5 minutes. Shape into 6 oval patties.

3 Lightly spray large nonstick skillet with nonstick cooking spray. Cook salmon cakes over medium heat 3 to 4 minutes on each side or until golden brown and heated through. Serve with sauce.

Makes 6 servings

Taco Loaf

MEATLOAF

- 1½ pounds 80% lean ground beef
- ¾ cup **QUAKER® Oats** (quick or old fashioned, uncooked)
- ½ cup thick and chunky salsa
- 1 egg, lightly beaten
- 1 packet (1 to 1.25 ounces) reduced-sodium taco seasoning mix

TOPPINGS

- ¾ cup thick and chunky salsa
- ½ cup (2 ounces) shredded reduced-fat Cheddar cheese
- 1½ cups shredded lettuce
- ½ cup chopped tomato
- ½ cup sliced ripe olives
- Reduced-fat sour cream (optional)

1 Heat oven to 350°F. Combine beef, oats, ½ cup salsa, egg and seasoning mix in large bowl; mix lightly but thoroughly. Press mixture evenly into 8- or 9-inch square metal baking pan.

2 Bake 40 to 45 minutes to medium doneness or until thermometer inserted into center of meatloaf registers 160°F and juices show no pink color. Drain any juices.

3 Top with ¾ cup salsa and sprinkle with cheese. Bake 5 minutes or until cheese has melted.

4 Let meatloaf stand 5 minutes before slicing. To serve, cut meatloaf into 6 squares. Top with lettuce, tomato, olives and sour cream, if desired.

Makes 6 servings

Spicy Oat-Crusted Chicken with Sunshine Salsa

SUNSHINE SALSA
- ¾ cup prepared salsa
- ¾ cup coarsely chopped orange sections

CHICKEN
- 2 tablespoons canola oil
- 1 tablespoon margarine, melted
- 2 teaspoons chili powder
- 1 teaspoon garlic powder

- 1 teaspoon ground cumin
- ¾ teaspoon salt
- 1½ cups **QUAKER® Oats** (quick or old fashioned, uncooked)
- 1 egg, lightly beaten
- 1 tablespoon water
- 4 boneless skinless chicken breasts (about 5 to 6 ounces each)
- Chopped fresh cilantro (optional)

1 Combine salsa and orange sections in small bowl. Cover and chill.

2 Heat oven to 375°F. Line baking sheet with aluminum foil. Stir together oil, margarine, chili powder, garlic powder, cumin and salt in flat, shallow dish. Add oats, stirring until evenly moistened.

3 Beat egg and water with fork until frothy in second flat, shallow dish. Dip chicken into egg mixture, then coat completely in seasoned oats. Place chicken on foil-lined baking sheet. Pat any extra oat mixture onto top of chicken.

4 Bake 30 minutes or until chicken is cooked through and oat coating is golden brown. Serve with salsa. Garnish with cilantro, if desired.

Makes 4 servings

Meatball Veggie Kabobs

1 each green and red bell pepper, stems and seeds removed, cut into 1¼-inch pieces

1 yellow squash, cut lengthwise in half and then into 1¼-inch pieces

¼ cup reduced-fat vinaigrette-style Caesar salad dressing, divided

1 pound 90% lean ground beef

¾ cup **QUAKER® Oats** (quick or old fashioned, uncooked)

1 egg, lightly beaten

¼ cup fat-free (skim) milk

3 tablespoons finely chopped onion

1 tablespoon finely chopped garlic

1 teaspoon dried thyme leaves

1 teaspoon salt

½ teaspoon black pepper

Shredded Parmesan cheese (optional)

1 Heat broiler. Lightly spray rack of broiler pan with nonstick cooking spray. If using bamboo skewers, soak skewers in water. Toss bell peppers and squash with 2 tablespoons dressing in medium bowl. Set aside.

2 Combine beef, oats, egg, milk, onion, garlic, thyme, salt and pepper in large bowl; mix lightly but thoroughly. Shape mixture into 20 meatballs, about 1½ inches in diameter. Alternately thread meatballs and vegetables onto eight 12-inch bamboo or metal skewers. Arrange kabobs on broiler pan. Drizzle with any dressing remaining in medium bowl.

3 Broil 3 to 4 inches from heat, until meatballs are cooked through (160°F) and vegetables are tender, about 10 minutes, turning once and brushing with remaining 2 tablespoons dressing.

4 Serve kabobs sprinkled with cheese, if desired.

Makes 4 servings

Smart Lunch & Dinner Dishes

Garden Salmon Loaf

SAUCE

¾ cup frozen peas, thawed

¾ cup low-fat plain yogurt

1 tablespoon Dijon-style mustard

1 tablespoon chopped fresh dill weed or 1 teaspoon dried dill

Black pepper, to taste

SALMON LOAF

2 cans (15½ ounces each) salmon, drained, skin and bones removed

1 cup shredded carrots

1 cup **QUAKER®** Oats (quick or old fashioned, uncooked)

1 cup low-fat plain yogurt

¾ cup sliced green onions

1 can (2½ ounces) sliced ripe olives (optional)

3 egg whites, lightly beaten

⅓ cup chopped green bell pepper

1 tablespoon Dijon-style mustard

¼ teaspoon black pepper

1 For sauce, combine peas, yogurt, mustard, dill and pepper in small bowl; mix well. Cover and chill.

2 Heat oven to 350°F. Spray 8×4-inch or 9×5-inch loaf pan with nonstick cooking spray.

3 For loaf, combine salmon, carrots, oats, yogurt, green onions, olives, if desired, egg whites, bell pepper, mustard and pepper in large bowl; mix lightly but thoroughly. Press into prepared pan. Bake 50 to 60 minutes or until light golden brown. Let stand 5 minutes before slicing. Serve immediately with sauce.

Makes 10 servings

Meatloaf Focaccia Sandwich

SPREAD

- 1 ounce sun-dried tomatoes (not in oil)
- ½ cup fat-free or reduced-fat mayonnaise
- 1 clove garlic, minced
- Dash hot pepper sauce

MEATLOAF

- 1½ pounds lean ground beef or ground turkey breast
- ¾ cup **QUAKER® Oats** (quick or old fashioned, uncooked)
- ½ cup thinly sliced green onions

- ½ cup fat-free (skim) milk
- 1 egg, lightly beaten
- 1 teaspoon dried thyme leaves
- 1 teaspoon salt
- ½ teaspoon black pepper

SANDWICH FIXINGS

- 1 loaf focaccia bread, about 8×10 inches in diameter (about 1½ pounds)
- 8 slices reduced-fat Swiss or part-skim mozzarella cheese
- 8 large lettuce leaves

1 Heat oven to 350°F. For spread, soften tomatoes according to package directions; coarsely chop. Combine tomatoes, mayonnaise, garlic and hot pepper sauce in small bowl; mix well. Cover and chill.

2 For meatloaf, combine beef, oats, green onions, milk, egg, thyme, salt and pepper in large bowl; mix lightly but thoroughly. Press mixture evenly into 9×5-inch metal loaf pan.

3 Bake 60 to 75 minutes to medium doneness or until thermometer inserted into center of meatloaf registers 160°F for beef, 170°F for turkey, and juices show no pink color. Drain any juices. Let stand 5 minutes before slicing.

4 To serve, cut focaccia into 8 rectangles; cut each rectangle in half horizontally. Spread 1 tablespoon spread on inside surfaces of each focaccia piece. Cut meatloaf into 8 slices; place on half of focaccia rectangles. Top with cheese and lettuce; cover with remaining pieces of focaccia. Serve warm.

Makes 8 servings

Mini Meatloaf Boats

MEATLOAF

- 1½ pounds lean ground beef
- 1 cup tomato juice
- ¾ cup **QUAKER® Oats** (quick or old fashioned, uncooked)
- ¼ cup chopped onion
- 1 egg, lightly beaten
- 4 to 6 teaspoons Mexican seasoning blend

"SAILS"

- 6 thin pretzel sticks
- 3 slices American cheese, halved diagonally

  Salsa or catsup, as desired

1 Heat oven to 350°F.

2 Combine meatloaf ingredients in large bowl; mix lightly but thoroughly. Divide mixture into 6 equal parts. Shape each into 4×2¾-inch oval loaf on rack of broiler pan. Press back of measuring tablespoon into top of each loaf to form pocket. (After baking, pocket will hold salsa.)

3 Bake 25 to 28 minutes or until meatloaves are medium doneness (160°F) and centers are no longer pink. Remove from oven. Drain off any juices.

4 Form "sails" by carefully inserting pretzel sticks into cheese. Attach "sails" to meatloaves and fill pockets with salsa.

Makes 6 servings

Mu Shu Meatball Wraps

MEATBALLS

- **1** pound lean ground turkey or lean ground beef
- **¾** cup **QUAKER® Oats** (quick or old fashioned, uncooked)
- **½** cup finely chopped water chestnuts
- **⅓** cup chopped green onions
- **1** clove garlic, minced
- **1** teaspoon finely chopped fresh ginger or ¼ teaspoon ground ginger

- **¼** cup light soy sauce
- **1** tablespoon water

WRAPS

- **¾** cup prepared plum sauce
- **6** (10-inch) flour tortillas, warmed
- **1½** cups coleslaw mix or combination of shredded cabbage and shredded carrots

1 Heat oven to 350°F. Combine all meatball ingredients in large bowl; mix lightly but thoroughly. Shape into 24 (1½-inch) meatballs; arrange on rack of broiler pan.

2 Bake 20 to 25 minutes or until no longer pink in centers (170°F for turkey; 160°F for beef).

3 To prepare wraps, spread plum sauce on flour tortilla; add about ¼ cup coleslaw mix and 4 hot meatballs. Fold sides of tortilla to center, overlapping edges; fold bottom and top of tortilla under, completely enclosing filling. Repeat with remaining ingredients. Cut wraps in half to serve.

Makes 6 servings

Spinach-Stuffed Turkey Meatloaf

1 cup coarsely chopped mushrooms

¼ cup chopped onion

1 package (10 ounces) frozen chopped spinach, thawed and drained

½ cup (2 ounces) shredded part-skim mozzarella cheese, divided

¼ cup grated Parmesan cheese

1 pound 99% lean ground turkey breast

¾ cup **QUAKER® Oats** (quick or old fashioned, uncooked)

½ cup fat-free (skim) milk

1 egg white, lightly beaten

1 teaspoon Italian seasoning blend

½ teaspoon salt (optional)

¼ teaspoon black pepper

1 Heat oven to 375°F. Lightly spray medium skillet with nonstick cooking spray. Cook mushrooms and onion over medium-low heat 4 minutes or until onion is tender; remove from heat. Add spinach, ¼ cup mozzarella cheese and Parmesan cheese; mix well. Set aside.

2 Combine turkey, oats, milk, egg white, Italian seasoning, salt, if desired, and pepper in large bowl; mix lightly but thoroughly. Spoon ⅔ of mixture lengthwise down center of 11×7-inch glass baking dish. Form deep indentation down middle; fill indentation with reserved spinach mixture. Top with remaining turkey mixture, forming loaf. Seal edges to completely enclose spinach filling.

3 Bake 30 to 35 minutes or until thermometer inserted into center of meatloaf registers 170°F and juices show no pink color. Remove from oven; sprinkle with remaining ¼ cup mozzarella cheese. Return to oven 1 to 2 minutes or until cheese melts. Let stand 5 minutes before slicing.

Makes 8 servings

•Tip

If ground turkey breast is not available, 1 pound 90% lean ground turkey may be substituted. Proceed as recipe directs.

Stuffed Turkey Burgers with Smoky Aïoli

AÏOLI

- ½ cup 93% fat-free mayonnaise
- 1 canned chipotle pepper in adobo sauce, seeded, minced
- ¾ teaspoon adobo sauce (from can above)
- 1 clove garlic, minced

BURGERS

- 1½ pounds lean ground turkey
- 1 cup **QUAKER® Oats** (quick or old fashioned, uncooked)
- 3 cloves garlic, minced
- 2 tablespoons Worcestershire sauce

- 1½ teaspoons dried oregano leaves
- 1 teaspoon salt
- ½ teaspoon black pepper
- 6 fresh mozzarella balls (⅓ to ½ ounce each)
- 6 whole-wheat hamburger buns, split and lightly toasted
- ¾ cup jarred roasted red pepper halves, drained
- 1 bunch watercress, arugula or other favorite salad greens, stems removed

1 For aïoli, combine mayonnaise, chipotle pepper, adobo sauce and garlic in small bowl; mix well. Chill at least 30 minutes.

2 Heat grill or broiler.

3 For burgers, combine turkey, oats, garlic, Worcestershire sauce, oregano, salt and pepper in large bowl; mix lightly but thoroughly. Shape into 6 large patties, about ¼-inch thick. Place 1 mozzarella ball in center of each patty; shape burger mixture around cheese to completely enclose; reshape into patty.

4 Grill or broil 4 inches from heat 5 minutes on each side or until centers are no longer pink (170°F). Arrange burgers on bottom halves of buns; top with aïoli, roasted pepper pieces, watercress and bun tops.

Makes 6 servings

•Tip

If small fresh mozzarella balls are unavailable, substitute large fresh mozzarella balls, cut into ⅓- to ½-ounce pieces. A 3-ounce chunk of part-skim mozzarella cheese, cut into 6 pieces, can be substituted for fresh mozzarella.

Satisfying Soups & Sides

Traditional Stuffing

2 cups sliced celery

1 cup chopped onion

1½ tablespoons poultry seasoning

1 teaspoon sage

½ teaspoon salt

¼ teaspoon black pepper

2 tablespoons olive oil

8 cups fresh bread cubes (white, whole-wheat or multi-grain)

2 cups **QUAKER® Oats** (quick or old fashioned, uncooked)

1 cup chopped apple

1 cup dried cranberries

½ cup chopped walnuts

¼ cup chopped parsley

1 can (10¾ ounces) chicken broth

1 Cook celery, onion, poultry seasoning, sage, salt and pepper in oil over medium-low heat 4 to 5 minutes or until tender. Remove from heat.

2 Combine bread cubes, oats, apple, cranberries, walnuts and parsley; mix well.

3 Add onion mixture and chicken broth. Mix until bread is evenly coated.

4 Stuff into body and neck of turkey. Immediately after stuffing, place turkey in oven and begin roasting.

Makes 9 cups

•Tip

This is enough stuffing for a 13- to 19-pound turkey. If using a larger turkey, double the recipe and bake any remaining stuffing in a casserole dish for about 1 hour or until warmed through.

Asian Stuffed Mushrooms

24 large mushrooms (about 2 pounds)

½ cup reduced-sodium soy sauce

¼ cup dry sherry

½ pound ground turkey

¾ cup **QUAKER®** Oats (quick or old fashioned, uncooked)

½ cup sliced green onions

¼ cup finely chopped red or green bell pepper

1 egg white, lightly beaten

1 tablespoon Dijon-style mustard

2 cloves garlic, minced

1 Remove stems from mushrooms; reserve stems. Place mushroom caps in large bowl. Combine soy sauce and sherry in small bowl; pour over mushrooms. Cover and marinate at least 1 hour, stirring once after 30 minutes.

2 Finely chop reserved mushroom stems. Place in large bowl with turkey, oats, green onions, bell pepper, egg white, mustard and garlic; mix well. Drain mushroom caps, reserving marinade. Fill caps with turkey mixture, packing well and mounding slightly. Place on broiler pan. Brush tops with reserved marinade.

3 Broil 7 to 8 inches from heat 15 to 18 minutes or until turkey is cooked through. Serve immediately.

Makes 24 appetizers

Broccoli-Stuffed Tomatoes

4 large tomatoes (about 1 pound)

1 package (10 ounces) frozen chopped broccoli, thawed and well drained

⅔ cup **Old Fashioned QUAKER® Oats**, uncooked

½ cup low-fat small-curd cottage cheese

¼ cup chopped onion

1½ teaspoons minced fresh basil or ½ teaspoon dried basil leaves

1 clove garlic, minced

¼ cup finely shredded Parmesan or Swiss cheese

1 Heat oven to 350°F. Slice ¼ inch from stem end of each tomato. Scoop out pulp and seeds; discard or reserve for another use. Arrange tomatoes in shallow 1-quart glass baking dish.

2 Combine broccoli, oats, cottage cheese, onion, basil and garlic in medium bowl; mix well. Fill tomatoes with mixture; sprinkle with cheese.

3 Bake 20 to 25 minutes or until heated through.

Makes 4 servings

Quaker's Oatmeal Soup

1 onion, finely chopped (about ¾ cup)

½ cup shredded carrots

3 tablespoons butter or margarine, divided

½ cup **QUAKER® Oats** (quick or old fashioned, uncooked)

6 cups chicken broth

1 cup **QUAKER® Oats** (quick or old fashioned, cooked according to package directions)

Salt and black pepper, to taste

3 tablespoons finely chopped fresh parsley or 1 tablespoon dried parsley flakes

1 Cook onion and carrots in 2 tablespoons butter in large skillet or saucepan over medium-low heat, stirring often, 5 minutes or until onion is tender. Add uncooked oats and remaining 1 tablespoon butter. Cook, stirring often, 3 minutes or until oats are golden brown.

2 Stir in broth; bring to a low boil. Add cooked oatmeal, stirring until well mixed. Cook over medium heat 5 minutes. Season to taste with salt and pepper. Serve sprinkled with parsley.

Makes 4 servings

Hearty Meatball Stew

1 pound ground turkey breast or extra-lean ground beef

¾ cup **QUAKER® Oats** (quick or old fashioned, uncooked)

1 can (8 ounces) no-salt-added tomato sauce, divided

1½ teaspoons garlic powder

1½ teaspoons dried thyme leaves, divided

2 cans (14½ ounces each) 70% less sodium, fat-free chicken broth

¾ teaspoon salt (optional)

2½ cups any frozen vegetable blend (do not thaw)

⅓ cup ditalini or other small pasta, uncooked

¼ cup water

2 tablespoons cornstarch

1 Heat broiler. Lightly spray rack of broiler pan with nonstick cooking spray.

2 Combine turkey, oats, ⅓ cup tomato sauce, garlic powder and 1 teaspoon thyme in large bowl; mix lightly but thoroughly. Transfer to sheet of aluminum foil or waxed paper. Pat mixture into 9×6-inch rectangle. Cut into 1½-inch squares; roll each square into a ball. Arrange meatballs on broiler pan.

3 Broil meatballs 6 to 8 inches from heat about 6 minutes or until cooked through, turning once.

4 While meatballs cook, bring broth, remaining tomato sauce, remaining ½ teaspoon thyme and salt, if desired, to a boil in 4-quart saucepan or Dutch oven over medium-high heat. Add vegetables and pasta; return to a boil. Reduce heat, cover and simmer 10 minutes or until vegetables and pasta are tender. Stir together water and cornstarch in small bowl until smooth. Add to pan along with meatballs. Cook and stir until broth is thickened. Spoon into bowls.

Makes 6 servings

Satisfying Soups & Sides

ABC Meatball Soup

MEATBALLS

- 1 pound ground turkey breast or extra-lean ground beef
- ¾ cup **QUAKER® Oats** (quick or old fashioned, uncooked)
- ⅓ cup barbecue sauce or ketchup

SOUP

- 1 carton (48 ounces) reduced-sodium, fat-free chicken broth (about 6 cups)
- ¼ cup alphabet or other small shaped pasta, uncooked
- 1 package (10 ounces) frozen mixed vegetables (do not thaw)

1 Heat broiler. Lightly spray rack of broiler pan with nonstick cooking spray.

2 For meatballs, combine turkey, oats and barbecue sauce in large bowl; mix lightly but thoroughly. Transfer to sheet of foil. Pat mixture into 9×6-inch rectangle. Cut into 1½-inch squares; roll each square into ball to make 24 meatballs. Arrange on broiler pan.

3 Broil 6 to 8 inches from heat about 6 minutes or until cooked through, turning once.

4 For soup, bring broth to a boil in 4-quart saucepan or Dutch oven over medium-high heat. Add pasta and frozen vegetables; return to a boil. Reduce heat; cover and simmer 8 minutes or until vegetables and pasta are tender. Add meatballs and cook 1 minute. Serve immediately.

Makes 6 (1⅓-cup) servings

•Tips

Garlic powder, onion powder or dried thyme may be added to the meatball ingredients.

Frozen corn, frozen green beans, frozen peas and carrots, or your favorite vegetable blend may be substituted for the mixed vegetables.

Three Pepper Oat Pilaf

½ cup chopped red bell pepper

½ cup chopped yellow bell pepper

½ cup chopped mushrooms

½ cup sliced green onions

2 garlic cloves, minced

1 tablespoon olive oil

1¾ cups **Old Fashioned QUAKER®
Oats**, uncooked

2 egg whites or 1 egg, lightly
beaten

¾ cup low-fat chicken broth

2 tablespoons minced fresh basil
or 2 teaspoons dried basil
leaves

½ teaspoon salt

¼ teaspoon black pepper

1 Cook bell peppers, mushrooms, green onions and garlic in oil in
10-inch nonstick skillet over medium heat, stirring occasionally, until
vegetables are crisp-tender, about 2 minutes.

2 Mix oats and egg whites in large bowl until oats are evenly coated.
Add oats to vegetable mixture in skillet.

3 Cook over medium heat, stirring occasionally, until oats are dry and
separated, about 5 to 6 minutes. Add broth, basil, salt and pepper. Continue
cooking, stirring occasionally, 2 to 3 minutes or until liquid is absorbed.
Serve immediately.

Makes 6 servings

Oh-So-Good
Cookies
& Snacks

Chewy Oatmeal Spice Bars

¾ cup firmly packed brown sugar

½ cup granulated sugar

¼ cup (½ stick) margarine

¾ cup apple butter or applesauce

2 egg whites or 1 egg

2 tablespoons fat-free (skim) milk

2 teaspoons vanilla

1½ cups all-purpose flour

1 teaspoon baking soda

1 teaspoon ground cinnamon

½ teaspoon salt (optional)

¼ teaspoon ground nutmeg (optional)

3 cups **QUAKER® Oats** (quick or old fashioned, uncooked)

1 cup raisins or diced dried mixed fruit

1 Heat oven to 350°F. Lightly spray 13×9-inch baking pan with nonstick cooking spray.

2 Beat brown sugar, granulated sugar and margarine in large bowl until well blended. Add apple butter, egg whites, milk and vanilla; beat well. Add combined flour, baking soda, cinnamon, and, if desired, salt and nutmeg; mix well. Stir in oats and raisins; mix well. (Dough will be moist.) Press dough evenly onto bottom of baking pan.

3 Bake 30 to 35 minutes or until light golden brown. Cool completely in pan. Cut into bars. Store tightly covered.

Makes 32 bars

Pumpkin Spice Oatmeal Cookies

COOKIES

1 cup granulated sugar

½ cup (1 stick) 70% vegetable oil spread

1 cup canned pumpkin

2 egg whites or 1 egg

1 teaspoon grated orange peel

2 cups **QUAKER® Oats** (quick or old fashioned, uncooked)

1 cup all-purpose flour

1 teaspoon pumpkin pie spice or ground cinnamon

½ teaspoon baking soda

½ teaspoon salt

½ cup finely chopped pitted prunes

¼ cup finely chopped walnuts

GLAZE

½ cup powdered sugar

1 tablespoon **TROPICANA PURE PREMIUM® Orange Juice**

1 Heat oven to 350°F. Lightly spray cookie sheets with nonstick cooking spray.

2 For cookies, beat granulated sugar and spread in large bowl with electric mixer until well blended. Add pumpkin, egg whites and orange peel; beat well. (Mixture will look curdled.) Add combined oats, flour, pumpkin pie spice, baking soda and salt; mix well. Stir in prunes and walnuts. Drop dough by rounded measuring tablespoonfuls about 2 inches apart on cookie sheets.

3 Bake 11 to 13 minutes or until lightly browned. (Do not overbake. Centers of cookies will be soft.) Cool 1 minute on cookie sheets; remove to wire racks. Cool completely.

4 For glaze, combine powdered sugar and orange juice in small bowl; mix well. Drizzle glaze over cooled cookies. Let cookies stand until glaze sets. Store tightly covered.

Makes about 48 cookies

• Tip

To make your own pumpkin pie spice, combine 4 teaspoons ground cinnamon, 1 teaspoon ground ginger, ½ teaspoon ground allspice, ½ teaspoon ground cloves and ½ teaspoon ground nutmeg in a small container with a tight-fitting lid. Store in cool, dark cabinet.

Choc-Oat-Chip Cookies

1 cup (2 sticks) margarine or butter, softened
1 cup firmly packed brown sugar
½ cup granulated sugar
2 eggs
2 tablespoons milk
2 teaspoons vanilla
1¾ cups all-purpose flour
1 teaspoon baking soda
½ teaspoon salt (optional)
2½ cups **QUAKER® Oats** (quick or old fashioned, uncooked)
2 cups semisweet chocolate chips
1 cup coarsely chopped nuts (optional)

1 Heat oven to 375°F.

2 Beat together margarine and sugars until creamy. Add eggs, milk and vanilla; beat well. Add flour, baking soda and salt; mix well. Stir in oats, chocolate chips and nuts; mix well. Drop by rounded tablespoonfuls onto ungreased cookie sheets.*

3 Bake for 9 to 10 minutes for a chewy cookie or 12 to 13 minutes for a crisp cookie. Cool 1 minute on cookie sheets; remove to wire racks. Cool completely. Store in tightly covered container.

Makes about 5 dozen cookies

*For bar cookies: *Press dough evenly into ungreased 13×9-inch metal baking pan. Bake 30 to 35 minutes or until light golden brown. Cool completely; cut into bars. Store tightly covered.*

High altitude adjustment:
Increase flour to 2 cups.

Variations: Prepare cookies as recipe directs, except substitute 1 cup of any of the following for 1 cup chocolate chips: raisins, chopped dried apricots, dried cherries, crushed toffee pieces, candy-coated chocolate pieces or white chocolate baking pieces.

Spirited Southern Sweet Potato Bars

2 cups **QUAKER® Oats** (quick or old fashioned, uncooked)

1½ cups all-purpose flour

¼ teaspoon salt (optional)

⅛ to ¼ teaspoon ground red pepper

1 cup (2 sticks) butter or margarine, softened

⅔ cup granulated sugar

1 teaspoon vanilla

2 cups mashed cooked sweet potato or canned pumpkin

2 eggs, lightly beaten

¾ cup firmly packed brown sugar

2 tablespoons bourbon or ½ teaspoon rum extract

1 cup chopped pecans

1. Heat oven to 375°F. Lightly grease 13×9-inch baking pan.

2. Combine oats and flour in large bowl; mix well. Measure ⅔ cup of mixture into small bowl; stir in salt, if desired, and red pepper. Set aside.

3. Add butter, granulated sugar and vanilla to remaining oat mixture; blend with electric mixer on low to medium speed until crumbly. Reserve 1 cup for topping. Press remaining mixture evenly onto bottom of prepared pan. Bake 15 minutes; remove pan from oven.

4. Combine sweet potato, reserved ⅔ cup oat mixture, eggs, brown sugar and bourbon, if desired, in separate bowl; mix well. Spread filling over warm crust. Add pecans to reserved topping mixture; mix well. Sprinkle evenly over sweet potato filling.

5. Bake 30 to 35 minutes or until topping is light golden brown. Cool in pan on wire rack; cut into bars. Serve at room temperature. Store in refrigerator tightly covered.

Makes 32 bars

Oatmeal Gingerbread Cookies

1 cup (2 sticks) margarine or butter, softened
¾ cup firmly packed brown sugar
½ cup molasses
1 egg
3⅓ cups all-purpose flour
1½ cups **QUAKER® Oats** (quick or old fashioned, uncooked)

1 teaspoon ground cinnamon
1 teaspoon ground ginger
½ teaspoon ground nutmeg
½ teaspoon baking soda
¼ teaspoon salt (optional)
Ready-to-spread frosting
Assorted candies

1 Beat margarine and brown sugar in large bowl until creamy. Add molasses and egg; beat well. Add combined flour, oats, cinnamon, ginger, nutmeg, baking soda and salt, if desired; mix well. Cover; chill about 2 hours.

2 Heat oven to 350°F. On floured surface, roll dough out about ¼ inch thick for a chewy cookie or ⅛ inch thick for a crisp cookie. Cut with 5-inch gingerbread man or woman cookie cutter. Place on ungreased cookie sheets.

3 Bake 8 to 10 minutes or until set. Cool 1 minute on cookie sheets; remove to wire racks. Cool completely.

4 Frost and decorate cookies with candies. Store loosely covered at room temperature.

Makes 20 (5-inch) cookies

Double Cherry Oatmeal Cookie Bars

1 9×9-inch Oatmeal Cookie Crust (recipe follows)*
¾ cup sliced unblanched almonds
1 10- to 12-ounce jar cherry preserves or all-fruit cherry spread

1 tablespoon lemon juice
1 tablespoon kirsch** or ¼ teaspoon almond extract
1 cup dried cherries

*Reserve ¾ cup Oatmeal Cookie Crust when preparing.
**Kirsch is cherry-flavored brandy.

1 Heat oven to 375°F. Prepare Oatmeal Cookie Crust as instructed below. Bake crust 10 to 12 minutes or until light golden brown; cool on wire rack.

2 Stir almonds into the reserved ¾ cup oat mixture; set aside. In medium bowl, combine cherry preserves, lemon juice and kirsch. Stir in dried cherries; let stand 10 minutes. Spread cherry mixture evenly over crust. Sprinkle with the reserved oat-almond mixture; press lightly into cherry filling.

3 Bake 30 to 35 minutes or until nicely browned on top. Cool completely on wire rack. Cut into bars. Store tightly covered at room temperature or freeze.

Makes 24 bars

Oatmeal Cookie Crust

1½ cups **QUAKER®** Oats (quick or old fashioned, uncooked)
1 cup all-purpose flour
½ cup firmly packed brown sugar

½ teaspoon baking soda
¼ teaspoon salt (optional)
8 tablespoons (1 stick) plus 2 tablespoons butter, melted

1 Spray 9×9-inch baking pan with nonstick cooking spray.

2 In large bowl, combine oats, flour, brown sugar, baking soda and salt, if desired; mix well. Stir in butter; mix well. (Set aside ¾ cup of the oat mixture for topping.) Press remaining oat mixture onto bottom of pan.

Makes 1 crust

Oh-So-Good Cookies & Snacks

Loaded Up Oatmeal Cookies

1 cup trans-fat-free
vegetable shortening
or 1 cup (2 sticks)
butter, softened

¾ cup firmly packed brown
sugar

¾ cup granulated sugar

2 eggs

1 teaspoon vanilla

2 cups all-purpose flour

½ teaspoon baking soda

½ teaspoon salt
(optional)

¼ teaspoon baking
powder

2 cups **QUAKER® Oats** (quick or old fashioned, uncooked)

1½ cups semisweet chocolate chips

⅔ cup chopped nuts

⅔ cup shredded coconut

⅔ cup raisins

1 Heat oven to 350°F. Beat shortening and sugars in large bowl with electric mixer until creamy. Add eggs and vanilla; beat well. Add combined flour, baking soda, salt, if desired, and baking powder; mix well. Add oats, chocolate chips, nuts, coconut and raisins; mix well.

2 Drop dough by rounded tablespoonfuls onto ungreased cookie sheets; flatten slightly.

3 Bake 10 to 12 minutes or until light golden brown. Cool 2 minutes on cookie sheets; remove to wire racks. Cool completely. Store tightly covered.

Makes about 54 cookies

Coconut Oatmeal Biscotti

1 cup **QUAKER® Oats** (quick or old fashioned, uncooked)
1 cup shredded coconut
½ cup toasted chopped pecans
1¾ cups all-purpose flour
¾ cup firmly packed brown sugar

1½ teaspoons baking powder
½ teaspoon salt
¼ cup light coconut milk
1 teaspoon vanilla
2 large eggs
½ cup white chocolate chips

1 Preheat oven to 350°F. Line baking sheet with parchment paper. Set aside.

2 Combine oats, coconut and pecans in food processor; process until finely ground. Lightly spoon flour into dry measuring cups; level with knife. Combine oat mixture, flour, brown sugar, baking powder and salt in large bowl; mix well. Combine coconut milk, vanilla and eggs in small bowl; mix well. Add to dry ingredients all at once; stir just until dry ingredients are moistened.

3 Turn dough out onto floured surface; knead lightly seven times with floured hands. Shape dough into 15×3-inch log on prepared baking sheet; pat to 1-inch thickness.

4 Bake 30 minutes. Remove to wire rack to cool.

5 Cut roll diagonally into 18 (½-inch) slices. Place, cut sides down, on baking sheet. Reduce oven temperature to 325°F; bake 18 minutes. Turn cookies over; bake an additional 18 minutes. (Cookies will be slightly soft in center but will harden as they cool.) Remove to wire rack to cool completely.

6 Place white chocolate chips in small microwave-safe bowl; microwave on HIGH (100% power) 30 seconds or until almost melted, stirring until smooth. Spread evenly over tops of biscotti.

Makes 18 biscotti

Chocolate Chip Dulce de Leche Nachos

1 cup **QUAKER® Oats** (quick or old fashioned, uncooked)

½ cup plus 2 tablespoons all-purpose flour, divided

⅓ cup firmly packed light brown sugar

¾ teaspoon ground cinnamon

6 tablespoons butter, melted

⅓ cup chopped salted roasted almonds

½ cup dulce de leche or caramel sauce

4 (7-inch) flour tortillas

¾ cup semisweet chocolate chips

1 Heat oven to 375°F. Combine oats, ½ cup flour, brown sugar and cinnamon in medium bowl; mix well. Add butter; stir until evenly moistened. Stir in almonds. Set aside.

2 Stir together dulce de leche and remaining 2 tablespoons flour in small bowl until blended. Place tortillas on ungreased baking sheets. Spread each tortilla with dulce de leche mixture to within ½ inch of edge; sprinkle evenly with ½ cup chocolate chips, then oat topping. Sprinkle remaining ¼ cup chocolate chips over tortillas.

3 Bake 12 to 14 minutes, or until oat mixture is golden brown and tortilla is crisp on bottom. Cool at least 5 minutes. Cut each tortilla into 6 wedges. Serve warm or cool.

Makes 8 servings

Winter Trail Mix

2 cups **Old Fashioned QUAKER® Oats**, uncooked

1½ cups **QUAKER® Oatmeal Squares Cereal**

¼ cup maple-flavored syrup, regular or light

1 tablespoon vegetable oil

1 teaspoon vanilla

½ cup snipped dried apple chunks

½ cup snipped dried apricots

½ cup dried cranberries

¾ cup lightly salted almonds or dry-roasted peanuts

1 Heat oven to 325°F. Combine oats and cereal in large bowl. Combine maple syrup, oil and vanilla in small bowl; pour over cereal mixture. Mix until well coated. Transfer to 15×10-inch jelly-roll pan.

2 Bake 20 to 25 minutes until oats are golden brown, stirring every 10 minutes.

3 Remove from oven. Immediately stir in apples, apricots, cranberries and nuts. Cool completely in pan on wire rack. Store loosely covered up to 1 week.

Makes 12 servings

Serving Suggestions: • Spread a whole-grain bagel half with peanut butter; sprinkle with trail mix, pressing lightly into peanut butter. • Mix trail mix with light cream cheese; spread on whole-grain bagels or whole-wheat toast. • Stir trail mix into low-fat vanilla yogurt or low-fat cottage cheese for breakfast or a snack. • Make a crunchy breakfast parfait by layering trail mix with fresh fruit (sliced bananas, chopped apples, grape halves, pineapple chunks) and low-fat yogurt. • Serve cold with milk. • Stir trail mix into pancake batter before cooking. • Put individual servings of trail mix in resealable plastic bags to eat away from home.

Soft Oaty Pretzels

3 to 3½ cups all-purpose flour, divided

1½ cups **QUAKER® Oats** (quick or old fashioned, uncooked), divided

2 tablespoons granulated sugar

1 package (¼ ounce) quick-rising yeast (about 2¼ teaspoons)

1½ teaspoons salt

¾ cup milk

¾ cup water

2 tablespoons margarine or butter, softened

1 egg, lightly beaten

1 Combine 2 cups flour, 1¼ cups oats, sugar, yeast and salt in large bowl; mix well. Heat milk and water in small saucepan until very warm (120°F to 130°F); stir in margarine. Add to flour mixture. Blend with electric mixer at low speed until moistened; beat 3 minutes at medium speed. By hand, gradually stir in enough remaining flour to make soft dough that pulls away from sides of bowl.

2 Turn dough out onto lightly floured surface. Knead 5 to 8 minutes or until smooth and elastic, adding additional flour if dough is sticky. Cover loosely with plastic wrap; let dough rest on floured surface 10 minutes.

3 Heat oven to 350°F. Lightly grease or spray two large baking sheets with nonstick cooking spray.

4 Divide dough into 24 equal pieces. Roll each piece into 12-inch-long rope; form into pretzel, letter or number shape. Place on baking sheets. Cover loosely with plastic wrap; let rest 10 minutes or until slightly risen. Brush tops of pretzel with beaten egg; sprinkle with remaining ¼ cup oats, pressing lightly.

5 Bake 15 to 18 minutes or until golden brown. (If baking both sheets at one time, rotate sheets top to bottom and front to back halfway through baking time.) Remove from baking sheets; cool on wire racks. Store tightly covered at room temperature.

Makes 24 pretzels

Fruit and Honey Oatmeal Bars

¼ cup honey
¼ cup (½ stick) margarine or
   butter
3 tablespoons granulated sugar
¼ teaspoon ground cinnamon
1½ cups crispy rice cereal

1 package (6 ounces) diced dried
   mixed fruit (about 1⅓ cups)
1 cup **QUAKER® Oats** (quick or
   old fashioned, uncooked)

1 Heat honey, margarine, sugar and cinnamon in medium saucepan over medium-low heat until margarine is melted, stirring frequently. Bring to a boil; cook 1 minute, stirring constantly. Remove from heat. Stir in rice cereal, dried fruit and oats until evenly coated.

2 Press mixture evenly onto bottom of ungreased 8-inch square baking pan. Cool completely. Cut into bars. Store tightly covered in refrigerator.

Makes 16 bars

3-Minute No-Bake Cookies

2 cups granulated sugar
½ cup (1 stick) margarine or
   butter
½ cup reduced-fat (2%) milk

⅓ cup unsweetened cocoa
   powder
3 cups **QUAKER® Oats** (quick or
   old fashioned, uncooked)

In large saucepan, combine sugar, margarine, milk and cocoa. Bring to a boil over medium heat, stirring frequently. Continue boiling 3 minutes. Remove from heat. Stir in oats; mix well. Quickly drop by tablespoonfuls onto waxed paper or greased cookie sheet. Let stand until set. Store tightly covered at room temperature.

Makes about 3 dozen cookies

Triple Peanut Butter Oatmeal Bars

1½ cups firmly packed
    brown sugar

1 cup peanut butter

½ cup (1 stick) margarine
    or butter, softened

2 large eggs

1 teaspoon vanilla

2 cups **QUAKER®**
    Oats (quick or old
    fashioned, uncooked)

1 cup all-purpose flour

½ teaspoon baking soda

1 bag (8 ounces) candy-
    coated peanut butter
    pieces

½ cup chopped peanuts

1 Heat oven to 350°F. Lightly spray 13×9-inch baking pan with nonstick cooking spray.

2 Beat brown sugar, peanut butter and margarine in large bowl with electric mixer until creamy. Add eggs and vanilla; beat well. Add combined oats, flour and baking soda; mix well. Stir in peanut butter pieces. Spread dough evenly into pan. Sprinkle with peanuts, pressing in lightly with fingers.

3 Bake 35 to 40 minutes or just until center is set. Cool completely on wire rack. Cut into bars. Store tightly covered.

Makes 32 bars

Whole Grain Banana Fruit 'n' Nut Bars

1¼ cups whole wheat flour	1 large egg
2 teaspoons pumpkin pie spice	1¼ cups mashed ripe bananas (about 3 small bananas)
½ teaspoon baking soda	
¼ teaspoon salt	1½ cups **QUAKER® Oats** (quick or old fashioned, uncooked)
½ cup (1 stick) light butter	
⅔ cup firmly packed brown sugar	⅔ cup chopped pitted dates or golden raisins
	⅔ cup chopped toasted walnuts

1 Heat oven to 350°F. Lightly spray 13×9×2-inch metal baking pan with nonstick cooking spray. Stir together flour, pumpkin pie spice, baking soda and salt in medium bowl; mix well. Set aside.

2 Beat butter and brown sugar in large bowl with electric mixer until well blended. Add egg and bananas; mix well. (Mixture will look curdled.) Add flour mixture; beat on low just until well blended. Stir in oats, dates and walnuts. Spread evenly in prepared pan.

3 Bake 20 to 25 minutes, until edges are golden brown and wooden pick inserted in center comes out with a few moist crumbs clinging to it. Cool completely in pan on wire rack. Cut into bars.

Makes 24 bars

Note: To store, wrap tightly in foil and store up to 2 days at room temperature. For longer storage, label and freeze in airtight container up to 3 months. Defrost, uncovered, at room temperature.

• Tip

To toast nuts, spread in single layer on cookie sheet. Bake at 350°F about 6 to 8 minutes or until lightly browned and fragrant, stirring occasionally. Cool before using. Or, spread in single layer on microwave-safe plate. Microwave on HIGH (100% power) 1 minute; stir. Continue to microwave on HIGH, checking every 30 seconds, until nuts are fragrant and brown. Cool before using.

Peanutty Crisscrosses

1½ cups firmly packed brown sugar
1 cup peanut butter
¾ cup (1½ sticks) margarine or butter, softened
⅓ cup water
1 egg

1 teaspoon vanilla
3 cups **QUAKER® Oats** (quick or old fashioned, uncooked)
1½ cups all-purpose flour
½ teaspoon baking soda
Granulated sugar

1 Beat brown sugar, peanut butter and margarine until creamy. Add water, egg and vanilla; beat well. Add combined oats, flour and baking soda. Cover; chill about 2 hours.

2 Heat oven to 350°F. Shape dough into 1-inch balls. Place 2 inches apart on ungreased cookie sheets; flatten with tines of fork, dipped in granulated sugar, to form crisscross pattern. Bake 9 to 10 minutes or until edges are golden brown. Cool 2 minutes on cookie sheets; remove to wire racks. Cool completely. Store tightly covered.

Makes about 7 dozen cookies

Oh-So-Good Cookies & Snacks

Terrific Trail Mix

3 cups **QUAKER® Oatmeal Squares Cereal**

1½ cups **QUAKER® Oats** (quick or old fashioned, uncooked)

⅓ cup roasted salted soy nuts or dry-roasted peanuts

¼ cup honey

2 tablespoons vegetable oil

1 cup mixed dried fruit bits

½ cup mini candy-coated milk chocolate candies

1 Heat oven to 350°F. Spray 15×10-inch jelly-roll pan with nonstick cooking spray.

2 Combine cereal, oats and soy nuts in large bowl. Combine honey and oil in small bowl; mix well. Add to cereal mixture; mix well. Spread mixture in single layer on prepared baking sheet.

3 Bake 12 to 15 minutes, stirring three times during baking. Remove from oven; stir to loosen mix from pan. Cool completely in pan on wire rack. Stir in dried fruit and candy. Store tightly covered.

Makes about 7 cups

Berry Berry Streusel Bars

1½ cups **QUAKER® Oats** (quick or old fashioned, uncooked)

1¼ cups all-purpose flour

½ cup firmly packed brown sugar

¾ cup (1½ sticks) butter or margarine, melted

1 cup fresh or frozen blueberries (do not thaw)

⅓ cup raspberry or strawberry preserves

1 teaspoon all-purpose flour

½ teaspoon grated lemon peel (optional)

1 Heat oven to 350°F. Combine oats, flour, brown sugar and butter; mix until crumbly. Reserve 1 cup oat mixture for topping. Set aside. Press remaining mixture onto bottom of ungreased 8- or 9-inch square baking pan. Bake 13 to 15 minutes or until light golden brown. Cool slightly.

2 Combine blueberries, preserves, flour and lemon peel, if desired, in medium bowl; mix gently. Spread over crust. Sprinkle with reserved oat mixture, patting gently.

3 Bake 20 to 22 minutes or until light golden brown. Cool completely. Cut into bars. Store tightly covered.

Makes 16 bars

1 cup firmly packed brown sugar

1 egg

½ cup vegetable oil, preferably canola

½ cup unsweetened applesauce

1 teaspoon vanilla

¾ cup whole-wheat flour

½ cup all-purpose flour

1 teaspoon baking soda

½ teaspoon salt

2 cups **QUAKER Oats®** (quick or old fashioned, uncooked)

1 cup "mix-ins" (dried cranberries, mixed dried fruit pieces, raisins, mini chocolate chips or chopped nuts)

1 Heat oven to 350°F. In large bowl, beat brown sugar, egg, oil, applesauce and vanilla on medium speed of electric mixer until combined. Add combined flours, baking soda and salt; beat on low speed just until blended. Stir in oats and "mix-ins."

2 Drop by dough by level measuring tablespoonfuls about 2 inches apart onto ungreased cookie sheets.

3 Bake 9 to 10 minutes, until light brown. (Do not overbake. Centers will appear soft.) Cool 1 to 2 minutes on cookie sheets; transfer to wire racks. Cool completely. Store tightly covered.

Makes about 36 cookies

Chewy Choc-Oat-Chip Bars

1 cup (2 sticks) margarine
    or butter, softened
1 cup firmly packed brown
    sugar
½ cup granulated sugar
2 eggs
2 tablespoons milk
2 teaspoons vanilla
1¾ cups all-purpose flour
1 teaspoon baking soda
½ teaspoon salt (optional)
2½ cups **QUAKER® Oats**
    (quick or old fashioned,
    uncooked)
2 cups (12 ounces) semisweet
    chocolate chips
1 cup chopped nuts (optional)

1 Heat oven to 375°F. Beat margarine and sugars in large bowl with electric mixer until creamy. Add eggs, milk and vanilla; beat well. Add combined flour, baking soda and salt, if desired; mix well. Stir in oats, chocolate chips and nuts, if desired; mix well. Press dough onto bottom of ungreased 13×9-inch baking pan.

2 Bake 30 to 35 minutes or until light golden brown. Cool completely, cut into bars. Store tightly covered.

Makes 32 bars

Variation: Substitute 1 cup of any of the following for 1 cup chocolate chips: candy-coated chocolate pieces, candy-coated peanut butter pieces, white chocolate chips, peanut butter & milk chocolate chips or butterscotch chips. Drop dough by rounded tablespoonfuls onto ungreased cookie sheets. Bake 9 to 10 minutes for a chewy cookie or 12 to 13 minutes for a crisp cookie. Cool 1 minute on cookie sheets; transfer to wire racks. Cool completely. Store tightly covered. Makes about 60 cookies.

Chewy Chocolate No-Bakes

1 cup (6 ounces) semisweet chocolate chips
5 tablespoons light butter
14 large marshmallows
1 teaspoon vanilla

2 cups **QUAKER® Oats** (quick or old fashioned, uncooked)
⅔ cup (any combination of) raisins, diced dried mixed fruit, shredded coconut, miniature marshmallows or chopped nuts

1 Melt chocolate chips, butter and large marshmallows in large saucepan over low heat, stirring until smooth. Remove from heat; cool slightly. Stir in vanilla. Stir in oats and remaining ingredients.

2 Drop by rounded tablespoonfuls onto waxed paper. Cover and refrigerate 2 to 3 hours. Let stand at room temperature about 15 minutes before serving. Store, tightly covered, in refrigerator.

Makes about 36 treats

Microwave Directions: Place chocolate chips, butter and marshmallows in large microwave-safe bowl. Microwave on HIGH (100% power) 1 to 2 minutes or until mixture is melted and smooth, stirring every 30 seconds. Proceed as directed.

Vanishing Oatmeal Raisin Cookies

½ cup (1 stick) plus
6 tablespoons butter,
softened

¾ cup firmly packed brown
sugar

½ cup granulated sugar

2 eggs

1 teaspoon vanilla

1½ cups all-purpose flour

1 teaspoon baking soda

1 teaspoon ground cinnamon

½ teaspoon salt (optional)

3 cups **QUAKER® Oats** (quick
or old fashioned, uncooked)

1 cup raisins

1 Heat oven to 350°F. Beat butter and sugars in large bowl with electric mixer on medium speed until creamy. Add eggs and vanilla; beat well. Add combined flour, baking soda, cinnamon and salt, if desired; mix well. Add oats and raisins; mix well.

2 Drop dough by rounded tablespoonfuls onto ungreased cookie sheets.

3 Bake 8 to 10 minutes or until light golden brown. Cool 1 minute on cookie sheets; remove to wire racks. Cool completely. Store tightly covered.

Makes 48 cookies

Variations: Stir in 1 cup chopped nuts. Substitute 1 cup semisweet chocolate chips or candy-coated chocolate pieces for raisins; omit cinnamon. Substitute 1 cup diced dried mixed fruit.

Bar Cookies: Press dough onto bottom of ungreased 13×9-inch baking pan. Bake 30 to 35 minutes or until light golden brown. Cool completely in pan on wire rack. Cut into bars. Store tightly covered. Makes 24 bars.

High-Altitude Adjustment: Increase flour to 1¾ cups and bake as directed.

Chocolate Peanut Butter Scrumpets

SCRUMPETS

- 1 cup all-purpose flour
- 1 cup **QUAKER® Oats** (quick or old fashioned, uncooked)
- 2 teaspoons baking powder
- 6 tablespoons butter or margarine, chilled and cut into pieces
- ½ cup semisweet chocolate chips
- ½ cup creamy peanut butter
- ½ cup honey
- ½ cup milk
- 1 egg
- 1 teaspoon vanilla

GLAZE

- ¼ cup honey
- ¼ cup unsweetened cocoa powder
- 1 to 2 tablespoons warm water

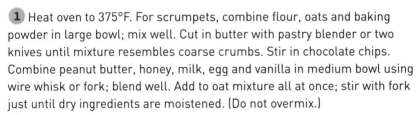

1 Heat oven to 375°F. For scrumpets, combine flour, oats and baking powder in large bowl; mix well. Cut in butter with pastry blender or two knives until mixture resembles coarse crumbs. Stir in chocolate chips. Combine peanut butter, honey, milk, egg and vanilla in medium bowl using wire whisk or fork; blend well. Add to oat mixture all at once; stir with fork just until dry ingredients are moistened. (Do not overmix.)

2 Spray measuring tablespoon with nonstick cooking spray. For each scrumpet, drop 2 heaping tablespoons dough in mounds 2 inches apart onto ungreased cookie sheets.

3 Bake 12 to 14 minutes or until golden brown. Remove to wire racks; cool 5 minutes.

4 For glaze, combine honey, cocoa and enough water to make pourable mixture in small bowl; blend well. Drizzle over scrumpets. Serve warm or at room temperature.

Makes 16 scrumpets

Oatmeal Macaroons

1 cup (2 sticks) margarine or butter, softened

1 cup firmly packed brown sugar

2 eggs

½ teaspoon almond extract

1¼ cups all-purpose flour

1 teaspoon baking soda

3 cups **QUAKER® Oats** (quick or old fashioned uncooked)

1 package (4 ounces) flaked or shredded coconut (about 1⅓ cups)

1 Heat oven to 350°F. Lightly grease cookie sheets.

2 Beat margarine and brown sugar in large bowl with electric mixer until creamy. Add eggs and almond extract; beat well. Add combined flour and baking soda; mix well. Add oats and coconut; mix well.

3 Drop dough by rounded teaspoonfuls onto prepared cookie sheets.

4 Bake 8 to 10 minutes or until light golden brown. Cool 2 minutes on cookie sheets; remove to wire racks. Cool completely. Store tightly covered.

Makes 48 cookies

Chocolate Coffee Toffee Oatmeal Cookies

½ to 1 teaspoon instant coffee powder

¼ cup boiling water

1⅓ cups firmly packed brown sugar

1 cup (2 sticks) 65% vegetable oil spread, softened

1 egg

1½ teaspoons vanilla

3 cups **QUAKER® Oats** (quick or old fashioned, uncooked)

1¼ cups all-purpose flour

¾ teaspoon salt

½ teaspoon baking soda

1 package (8 ounces) milk chocolate toffee bits (about 1⅓ cups)

1½ cups (8 ounces) semisweet chocolate chips

1 cup coarsely crumbled sugar cones (about 5 cones)

1 Heat oven to 350°F. Line cookie sheets with parchment paper or nonstick aluminum foil, or use nonstick cookie sheets.

2 Dissolve coffee in boiling water; cool to room temperature. Beat brown sugar and spread in large bowl with electric mixer at medium speed until creamy. Add egg; beat well. Beat in coffee and vanilla. Combine oats, flour, salt and baking soda in medium bowl; mix well. Gradually add to creamed mixture, beating well after each addition. Stir in toffee bits, chocolate chips and sugar cones. Drop dough by heaping measuring tablespoonfuls in mounds 2 inches apart onto prepared cookie sheets.

3 Bake 12 to 14 minutes, just until golden brown. Cool 1 minute on cookie sheets; remove to wire racks. Cool completely. Store loosely covered.

Makes about 60 cookies

Not-So-Sinful Brownies

¼ cup vegetable oil

3 squares (1 ounce each) unsweetened chocolate

1¼ cups granulated sugar

½ cup applesauce

4 egg whites or 2 eggs, lightly beaten

1 teaspoon vanilla

1 cup **QUAKER® Oats** (quick or old fashioned, uncooked)

1 cup all-purpose flour

1 teaspoon baking powder

¼ teaspoon salt (optional)

1 tablespoon powdered sugar

1 Heat oven to 350°F. Lightly spray bottom of 13×9-inch baking pan with nonstick cooking spray.

2 Heat oil and chocolate over low heat in large saucepan until chocolate is melted, stirring frequently. Remove from heat. Stir in granulated sugar and applesauce until sugar is dissolved. Stir in egg whites and vanilla until completely blended. Add combined oats, flour, baking powder and salt, if desired; mix well. Spread evenly into pan.

3 Bake 22 to 25 minutes or until edges begin to pull away from sides of pan. Cool completely in pan on wire rack. Cut into bars. Store tightly covered. Sprinkle with powdered sugar just before serving.

Makes 24 bars

Colossal Brownie Ice Cream Sandwich

TOPPING

⅓ cup **QUAKER® Oats** (quick or old fashioned, uncooked)

3 tablespoons all-purpose flour

2 tablespoons firmly packed brown sugar

⅓ cup peanut butter (not reduced fat)

1 tablespoon margarine or butter

BROWNIES

1 cup (6 ounces) semisweet chocolate chips

½ cup (1 stick) margarine or butter

¾ cup granulated sugar

1 teaspoon vanilla

2 eggs

1 cup all-purpose flour

¾ cup **QUAKER® Oats** (quick or old fashioned, uncooked)

½ teaspoon baking powder

¼ teaspoon salt (optional)

1 quart fat-free or low-fat vanilla ice cream or frozen yogurt, slightly softened

1 Heat oven to 350°F. Line two 8- or 9-inch round cake pans with aluminum foil, allowing foil to extend over sides of pans. Spray with nonstick cooking spray.

2 For topping, combine oats, flour and brown sugar in large bowl. Cut in peanut butter and margarine with pastry blender or two knives until mixture is crumbly. Set aside.

3 For brownies, melt chocolate chips and margarine in medium saucepan over low heat, stirring frequently. Remove from heat; cool slightly. Stir in granulated sugar and vanilla. Add eggs; mix well. Add combined flour, oats, baking powder and salt, if desired; mix well. Divide batter evenly between pans. Sprinkle with reserved topping, patting gently.

4 Bake 22 to 24 minutes for 8-inch pan (20 to 22 minutes for 9-inch pan) or just until center of brownie is set. (Do not overbake.) Cool completely in pans on wire rack.

5 To assemble, spread softened ice cream evenly over one brownie while still in pan. Lift second brownie out of pan; remove foil. With topping side up, place brownie on top of ice cream, pressing gently. Cover and freeze several hours or overnight. Remove from freezer 10 to 15 minutes before cutting. Lift from pan using foil edges. Remove foil; cut into wedges. Individually wrap wedges and store in freezer.

Makes 12 servings

Peanut Butter 'n' Fudge Filled Bars

1 cup (2 sticks) margarine or butter, softened

2 cups firmly packed brown sugar

¼ cup peanut butter

2 eggs

2 cups **QUAKER® Oats** (quick or old fashioned, uncooked)

2 cups all-purpose flour

1 teaspoon baking soda

¼ teaspoon salt (optional)

1 can (14 ounces) sweetened condensed milk (not evaporated milk)

2 cups (12 ounces) semisweet chocolate chips

2 tablespoons peanut butter

½ cup chopped peanuts

1 Heat oven to 375°F.

2 Beat margarine, brown sugar and ¼ cup peanut butter until creamy. Add eggs; beat well. Add combined oats, flour, baking soda and salt; mix well. Reserve 1 cup oat mixture for topping; set aside. Spread remaining oat mixture onto bottom of ungreased 13×9-inch baking pan.

3 In medium saucepan, combine condensed milk, chocolate chips and remaining 2 tablespoons peanut butter. Cook over low heat until chocolate is melted, stirring constantly. Remove from heat; stir in peanuts. Spread mixture evenly over crust. Drop reserved oat mixture by teaspoonfuls over chocolate mixture.

4 Bake 30 to 35 minutes or until light golden brown. Cool completely; cut into bars. Store tightly covered.

Makes 32 bars

Chewy Fruit and Oatmeal Bars

½ cup firmly packed brown sugar

½ cup granulated sugar

1 container (6 ounces) low-fat plain yogurt

1 egg, lightly beaten

2 tablespoons vegetable oil

2 tablespoons fat-free (skim) milk

2 teaspoons vanilla

1½ cups all-purpose flour

1 teaspoon baking soda

1 teaspoon ground cinnamon

½ teaspoon salt (optional)

3 cups **QUAKER® Oats** (quick or old fashioned, uncooked)

1 cup diced dried mixed fruit, raisins or dried cranberries

1 Heat oven to 350°F. Lightly spray bottom of 13×9-inch baking pan with nonstick cooking spray.

2 Combine sugars, yogurt, egg, oil, milk and vanilla in large bowl; mix well. Combine flour, baking soda, cinnamon, and salt, if desired, in medium bowl; mix well. Add to yogurt mixture; mix well. Stir in oats and dried fruit. Spread dough onto bottom of prepared pan.

3 Bake 22 to 25 minutes or until light golden brown. Cool completely on wire rack. Cut into bars. Store tightly covered.

Makes 24 bars

Cherry Berry Crisps

FILLING

½ cup granulated sugar

1 tablespoon cornstarch

½ cup cranberry juice or **TROPICANA PURE PREMIUM®** Orange Juice

2 cans (16 ounces each) pitted sour cherries, drained

⅓ cup dried cranberries

TOPPING

¾ cup **QUAKER® Oats** (quick or old fashioned, uncooked)

3 tablespoons firmly packed brown sugar

2 tablespoons margarine or butter, melted

1 tablespoon all-purpose flour

¼ teaspoon ground cinnamon

1 Heat oven to 375°F. For filling, stir together granulated sugar and cornstarch in medium saucepan. Gradually stir in cranberry juice, mixing well. Stirring constantly, bring to a boil over medium-high heat. Cook and stir 1 minute or until thickened and clear. Remove from heat; stir in cherries and cranberries. Spoon into six small (about 6-ounce) ovenproof heart-shaped ramekins, custard cups or soufflé cups, dividing evenly.

2 For topping, combine oats, brown sugar, margarine, flour and cinnamon in small bowl; mix well. Sprinkle topping over each fruit cup, dividing evenly.

3 Bake 15 to 20 minutes or until topping is golden brown. Serve warm.

Makes 6 servings

Variation: Spoon filling into an 8-inch square glass baking dish. Sprinkle evenly with topping. Bake 25 to 30 minutes or until topping is golden brown.

Show-Off
Desserts
& Cobblers

Fruit Crisp

FILLING

- 6 cups thinly sliced peeled apples, peaches or pears (6 to 8 medium)
- ¼ cup water
- ¼ cup firmly packed brown sugar
- 2 tablespoons all-purpose flour
- ½ teaspoon ground cinnamon

TOPPING

- ¾ cup **QUAKER® Oats** (quick or old fashioned, uncooked)
- 3 tablespoons firmly packed brown sugar
- 2 tablespoons margarine or light butter, melted
- ¼ teaspoon ground cinnamon
  Nonfat frozen yogurt (optional)

1 Heat oven to 350°F. Spray 8-inch square glass baking dish with nonstick cooking spray.

2 For filling, combine fruit and water in large bowl. Add brown sugar, flour and cinnamon; stir until fruit is evenly coated. Spoon into baking dish.

3 For topping, combine oats, brown sugar, margarine and cinnamon in medium bowl; mix well. Sprinkle evenly over fruit.

4 Bake 30 to 35 minutes or until fruit is tender. Serve warm with nonfat frozen yogurt, if desired.

Makes 8 servings

• Tip

If using apples, Jonathan, McIntosh, Winesap, Granny Smith, Northern Spy, Greening and Rome Beauty are recommended. One medium apple yields about 1 cup sliced or chopped. If using pears, Bartlett, Anjou and Bosc are recommended.

Snow Cakes

1 box (18.25 ounces) white cake mix without pudding

4 egg whites

1 cup (8 ounces) low-fat vanilla yogurt*

½ cup water

⅓ cup vegetable oil

1 cup **QUAKER® Oats** (quick or old fashioned, uncooked)

1 quart premium vanilla ice cream**

Yogurt containing gelatin is not recommended.

**Light/reduced-fat ice cream is not recommended.*

1 Heat oven to 350°F. Line 24 medium muffin pan cups with paper or foil liners.

2 Beat cake mix, egg whites, yogurt, water and oil in large bowl with electric mixer according to package directions. Gently fold in oats. Divide batter evenly among muffin cups, filling each about ¾ full.

3 Bake 20 minutes or until wooden pick inserted in center comes out clean. Remove from pan; cool completely on wire rack.

4 Remove ice cream from freezer and allow to soften just enough so it can be mixed. Transfer to chilled bowl; stir just until ice cream is spreadable but still holds its shape. Working quickly, "frost" each cupcake with softened ice cream. Place frosted cupcakes on tray and return to freezer to firm up slightly, no more than 30 minutes.

Makes 24 cupcakes

Variation: Sprinkle frosted cupcakes with shredded coconut.

Apple Raspberry Crumb Cake

CRUMB CAKE

1½ cups all-purpose flour
¾ cup **QUAKER® Oats** (quick or old fashioned, uncooked)
¾ cup granulated sugar
1 teaspoon ground cinnamon
½ teaspoon baking powder
½ teaspoon baking soda
½ teaspoon ground nutmeg
¼ teaspoon salt (optional)
½ cup (1 stick) butter, chilled

¼ cup part-skim ricotta cheese
¾ cup nonfat or reduced-fat sour cream
2 egg whites, lightly beaten

FILLING

2 cups chopped peeled apple (about 2 medium)
⅓ cup seedless raspberry jam
⅔ teaspoon all-purpose flour
Powdered sugar

1 Heat oven to 350°F. Lightly grease or spray 9-inch springform pan or round metal cake pan with nonstick cooking spray.

2 For cake and topping, combine 1½ cups flour, oats, granulated sugar, cinnamon, baking powder, baking soda, nutmeg and salt, if desired, in large bowl; mix well. Cut in butter and ricotta cheese with pastry blender or two knives until crumbly. Reserve 1½ cups oat mixture for topping. Set aside.

3 Combine sour cream and egg whites in small bowl; add to remaining oat mixture, mixing just until moistened. Spread batter over bottom and ½ inch up sides of pan.

4 For filling, combine apples, jam and ⅔ teaspoon flour; spoon over cake. Sprinkle reserved oat mixture over fruit.

5 Bake 50 to 55 minutes or until golden brown and center is firm to touch. Sprinkle with powdered sugar. Serve warm.

Makes 12 servings

Fudgy Banana Oat Cake

TOPPING

- 1 cup **QUAKER® Oats** (quick or old fashioned, uncooked)
- ½ cup firmly packed brown sugar
- ¼ cup (½ stick) margarine or butter, chilled

FILLING

- 1 cup (6 ounces) semisweet chocolate chips
- ⅔ cup sweetened condensed milk (not evaporated milk)
- 1 tablespoon margarine or butter

CAKE

- 1 package (18.25 ounces) devil's food cake mix
- 1¼ cups mashed ripe bananas (about 3 large)
- ⅓ cup vegetable oil
- 3 eggs
  Banana slices (optional)
  Sweetened whipped cream (optional)

1 Heat oven to 350°F. Lightly grease bottom only of 13×9-inch baking pan or spray with nonstick cooking spray. For topping, combine oats and brown sugar. Cut in margarine until mixture is crumbly; set aside.

2 For filling, in small saucepan, heat chocolate chips, condensed milk and margarine over low heat until chocolate is melted, stirring occasionally. Remove from heat; set aside.

3 For cake, combine cake mix, bananas, oil and eggs in large mixing bowl. Blend at low speed of electric mixer until dry ingredients are moistened. Beat at medium speed 2 minutes. Spread batter evenly into prepared pan. Drop chocolate filling by teaspoonfuls evenly over batter. Sprinkle with reserved oat topping. Bake 40 to 45 minutes or until cake pulls away from sides of pan and topping is golden brown. Cool cake in pan on wire rack. Cut into squares. Garnish with banana slices and sweetened whipped cream, if desired.

Makes 15 servings

Caramel-Topped Cheesecakes with Oat-Pecan Crust

1½ cups **QUAKER® Oats** (quick or old fashioned, uncooked)

½ cup finely chopped pecans

1¼ cups firmly packed light brown sugar, divided

¼ cup (½ stick) butter or margarine, melted

2 packages (8 ounces each) cream cheese, softened

1 teaspoon vanilla

3 large eggs, at room temperature

½ cup sour cream

¾ cup butterscotch caramel topping

Sea salt

1 Heat oven to 375°F. Line 18 medium muffin cups with foil liners.

2 Combine oats, pecans, ½ cup brown sugar and butter in large bowl, blending well. Spoon about 2 tablespoons of mixture into bottom of each muffin cup, then press evenly and firmly to form crust. Bake 8 to 10 minutes, or until golden brown. Remove from oven and cool.

3 Reduce oven temperature to 325°F. Beat cream cheese in large bowl with electric mixer at medium-high speed until light and fluffy, scraping bowl occasionally. Add remaining ¾ cup brown sugar and vanilla; blend well. Add eggs, one at a time, beating just until blended. Add sour cream; mix well. Divide batter evenly among prepared muffin cups. Bake about 20 to 22 minutes, or just until set. Cool in pans on wire rack. Chill at least 2 hours.

4 Just before serving, top each individual cheesecake with scant tablespoon of butterscotch caramel topping (if too thick to spread, place in microwave for a few seconds to soften). Sprinkle on a few grains of sea salt and serve.

Makes 18 cheesecakes

Apple Berry Breakfast Crisp

FILLING

- 4 cups thinly sliced peeled apples (about 4 medium)
- 2 cups fresh or frozen blueberries or sliced strawberries
- ¼ cup firmly packed brown sugar
- ¼ cup frozen orange juice concentrate, thawed
- 2 tablespoons all-purpose flour
- 1 teaspoon ground cinnamon

TOPPING

- 1 cup **QUAKER® Oats** (quick or old fashioned, uncooked)
- ½ cup firmly packed brown sugar
- ⅓ cup (5 tablespoons plus 1 teaspoon) margarine or butter, melted
- 2 tablespoons all-purpose flour

1 Heat oven to 350°F. Spray 8-inch square glass baking dish with nonstick cooking spray. For filling, combine apples, berries, brown sugar, juice concentrate, flour and cinnamon in large bowl; stir until fruit is evenly coated. Spoon into baking dish.

2 For topping, combine oats, brown sugar, margarine and flour in medium bowl; mix until crumbly. Sprinkle evenly over fruit.

3 Bake 30 to 35 minutes or until apples are tender. Serve warm.

Makes 9 servings

•Tip

For a delicious dessert, serve warm with vanilla frozen yogurt.

All-American Fruit Crumble Pie

CRUST

1 cup **QUAKER® Oats** (quick or old fashioned, uncooked)

¼ cup firmly packed brown sugar

¾ cup all-purpose flour

½ cup (1 stick) light butter, melted

TOPPING

⅓ cup **QUAKER® Oats** (quick or old fashioned, uncooked)

¼ cup all-purpose flour

¼ cup firmly packed brown sugar

3 tablespoons margarine or butter, chilled

FILLING

2 cans (21 ounces each) apple or peach pie filling

½ cup raisins

½ teaspoon ground cinnamon

Ice cream, frozen yogurt or whipped cream (optional)

1 Heat oven to 375°F. Lightly spray 9-inch glass pie plate with nonstick cooking spray.

2 For crust, combine oats, brown sugar, flour and butter in large bowl; mix well. Press mixture evenly onto bottom and on sides of prepared pie plate. Bake 12 to 15 minutes or until golden brown.

3 For topping, combine oats, flour and brown sugar in small bowl; mix well. Cut in margarine with pastry blender or two knives until mixture is crumbly. Set aside.

4 For filling, combine pie filling, raisins and cinnamon in large bowl; mix well. Pour into crust. Sprinkle reserved topping evenly over filling.

5 Bake 25 to 30 minutes or until topping is golden brown. Serve with ice cream, frozen yogurt or whipped cream, if desired.

Makes 8 servings

Banana Pudding Parfaits

1 package (4-serving size) instant vanilla pudding mix

2 cups cold reduced-fat (2%) milk

2 medium ripe bananas, cut into ⅛-inch slices

2½ cups **QUAKER® LIFE® Original Cereal**

Whipped topping (optional)

1 Prepare pudding mix according to package directions using 2 cups milk.

2 Layer 2 tablespoons pudding, 4 to 5 banana slices and ¼ cup cereal in 12-ounce glass. Repeat layers. Top with 3 tablespoons pudding, 2 tablespoons cereal and, if desired, whipped topping.

3 Repeat, using remaining ingredients to make three more parfaits. Serve immediately.

Makes 4 servings

Substitution: Substitute five ready-to-eat vanilla pudding cups (3.5 ounces) for prepared instant pudding mix.

Variations: Substitute chocolate, banana or butterscotch pudding mix for vanilla. Substitute **QUAKER® LIFE® Toasted Cinnamon Cereal**. For mini parfaits, divide ingredients evenly among eight 6-ounce clear plastic cups.

Layers of Love Cakes

CUPCAKES

- 1 package (18.25 ounces) white cake mix, regular or with pudding
- 1½ cups fat-free (skim) milk
- ⅓ cup canola oil
- 3 large egg whites
- 1 teaspoon vanilla
- 1 cup **QUAKER® Oats** (quick or old fashioned, uncooked)

FILLING

- 2 ounces reduced-fat cream cheese, softened
- 3 tablespoons powdered sugar, plus additional for garnish
- ½ teaspoon vanilla
- 1 cup whipping cream
- 1¾ cups fresh or frozen raspberries, coarsely crushed

1 Heat oven to 350°F. Lightly spray 24 medium muffin cups with nonstick cooking spray.

2 For cupcakes, beat cake mix, milk, oil, egg whites and 1 teaspoon vanilla in large bowl with electric mixer at low speed 30 seconds to blend. Beat 2 minutes on medium speed, scraping bowl occasionally. Gently fold in oats. Divide batter evenly among muffin cups, filling each about ¾ full.

3 Bake 20 to 22 minutes or until wooden pick inserted in center comes out clean. Cool 2 minutes in pan. Remove from pan; cool completely on wire rack.

4 For filling, beat cream cheese, powdered sugar and ½ teaspoon vanilla with electric mixer at low speed until blended. Add whipping cream, gradually increasing mixer speed to high and beating until soft peaks form. (Do not overbeat.)

5 Slice cupcakes in half horizontally with serrated knife. Spread cut side of cupcake bottoms with heaping measuring teaspoonful crushed raspberries. Top with heaping measuring tablespoonful filling. Place cupcake tops, cut sides down, on top of filling, pressing gently. Sprinkle with powdered sugar and garnish with additional fresh berries, if desired. Cover and refrigerate leftover cupcakes up to 3 days.

Makes 24 cupcakes

• Tip

Cupcakes may be baked ahead and frozen in tightly covered container up to 1 month. To thaw, remove cupcakes from container to plate and let stand at room temperature 30 minutes.

Autumn Fruit Cobbler

3 large apples, cored and cut into ¼-inch wedges

2 medium-firm ripe Bartlett or Bosc pears, peeled, quartered and cored

⅓ cup dried cranberries

1 cup firmly packed light brown sugar, divided

2 tablespoons cornstarch

1½ teaspoons ground cinnamon, divided

1½ cups all-purpose flour

1 cup **QUAKER®** Oats (quick or old fashioned, uncooked)

2 teaspoons baking powder

¼ teaspoon salt

½ cup (1 stick) margarine or butter, chilled

⅔ cup reduced-fat (2%) milk

Vanilla ice cream (optional)

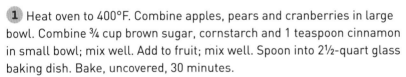

1 Heat oven to 400°F. Combine apples, pears and cranberries in large bowl. Combine ¾ cup brown sugar, cornstarch and 1 teaspoon cinnamon in small bowl; mix well. Add to fruit; mix well. Spoon into 2½-quart glass baking dish. Bake, uncovered, 30 minutes.

2 Combine flour, oats, remaining ¼ cup brown sugar, baking powder, salt and remaining ½ teaspoon cinnamon in large bowl; mix well. Cut in margarine with pastry blender or 2 knives until mixture resembles coarse crumbs. Add milk; mix with fork until soft dough forms. Turn out onto lightly floured surface; knead gently 6 to 8 times. Pat dough into ½-inch-thick rectangle. Cut with floured biscuit or cookie cutter.

3 Remove baking dish from oven; stir fruit. Carefully arrange biscuits over hot fruit; press lightly into fruit. Bake 15 to 20 minutes or until biscuits are golden brown and fruit mixture is bubbly. Serve warm with vanilla ice cream, if desired. Cover and refrigerate leftovers.

Makes 8 servings

Hidden Berry Cupcakes

1¾ cups all-purpose flour

1¼ cups granulated sugar

1 tablespoon baking powder

½ teaspoon salt

⅓ cup (5 tablespoons plus 1 teaspoon) butter, softened

3 eggs

⅔ cup milk

1 tablespoon vanilla

1 cup **QUAKER® Oats** (quick or old fashioned, uncooked)

½ cup seedless strawberry or raspberry fruit spread

Powdered sugar

1 Heat oven to 350°F. Line 16 medium muffin cups with paper or foil liners. Set aside.

2 Combine flour, granulated sugar, baking powder and salt in large bowl. Add butter and beat with electric mixer on low speed until crumbly, about 1 minute. Combine eggs, milk and vanilla in medium bowl; add to flour mixture. Beat on low speed until incorporated, then on medium speed 2 minutes. Gently fold in oats. Divide batter evenly among muffin cups, filling each about ¾ full.

3 Bake 18 minutes or until a wooden pick inserted in center comes out clean. Remove from pan; cool completely on wire rack.

4 Using small sharp knife, cut cone-shaped piece from center of each cupcake, leaving ¾-inch border around edge of cupcake. Carefully remove and reserve cake pieces. Fill each depression with generous teaspoon of fruit spread. Top with reserved cake pieces; sift powdered sugar over tops of cupcakes.

Makes 16 cupcakes

Easy Apple Custard Pie

CRUST

1¼ cups all-purpose flour

¾ cup **QUAKER® Oats** (quick or old fashioned, uncooked)

¼ cup firmly packed brown sugar

⅛ teaspoon salt (optional)

½ cup (1 stick) margarine or butter, melted

1 tablespoon water

1 teaspoon vanilla

FILLING

1 container (8 ounces) reduced-fat or regular sour cream

⅔ cup firmly packed brown sugar

¼ cup all-purpose flour

4 egg whites or 2 eggs, lightly beaten

½ teaspoon ground cinnamon

⅛ teaspoon ground nutmeg

4 cups thinly sliced peeled apples (4 to 5 medium)

TOPPING

¼ cup **QUAKER® Oats** (quick or old fashioned, uncooked)

¼ cup firmly packed brown sugar

¼ cup all-purpose flour

¼ cup (½ stick) margarine or butter, chilled and cut into pieces

1 Heat oven to 375°F. For crust, combine flour, oats, brown sugar and salt, if desired, in medium bowl; mix well. Add margarine, water and vanilla; mix well. Press firmly onto bottom and sides of 9-inch glass pie plate, forming ¼-inch rim around edge. Bake 12 to 15 minutes or until light golden brown. Cool completely on wire rack.

2 For filling, combine sour cream, brown sugar, flour, egg whites, cinnamon and nutmeg in medium bowl. Add apples; mix well. Spoon into cooled crust.

3 For topping, combine oats, brown sugar and flour in medium bowl; mix well. Cut in margarine with pastry blender or two knives until mixture resembles coarse crumbs. Sprinkle over filling.

4 Bake 50 to 60 minutes or until knife inserted in center comes out clean. Cool on wire rack. Serve warm or chilled. Store, tightly covered, in refrigerator.

Makes 8 servings

Lazy Daisy Oatmeal Cake

CAKE

1¼ cups boiling water
1 cup **QUAKER® Oats** (quick or old fashioned, uncooked)
1 cup granulated sugar
1 cup firmly packed brown sugar
5 tablespoons margarine or butter, softened
2 egg whites or 1 egg
1 teaspoon vanilla
1¾ cups all-purpose flour
1 teaspoon baking soda
1 teaspoon ground cinnamon
¼ teaspoon ground nutmeg (optional)
¼ teaspoon salt (optional)

TOPPING

½ cup shredded coconut
½ cup firmly packed brown sugar
½ cup **QUAKER® Oats** (quick or old fashioned, uncooked)
3 tablespoons fat-free (skim) milk
2 tablespoons margarine or butter, melted

1 Heat oven to 350°F. Lightly grease and flour 8- or 9-inch square baking pan.

2 For cake, pour boiling water over 1 cup oats in medium bowl; mix well. Set aside.

3 Beat granulated sugar, 1 cup brown sugar and 5 tablespoons margarine in large bowl until well blended. Add egg whites and vanilla; beat well. Add reserved oat mixture and combined flour, baking soda, cinnamon, and, if desired, nutmeg and salt; mix well. Pour batter into prepared pan.

4 Bake 55 to 65 minutes for 8-inch pan (50 to 60 minutes for 9-inch pan) or until wooden pick inserted in center comes out clean. Transfer cake in pan to wire rack.

5 For topping, combine all ingredients in small bowl; mix well. Spread evenly over top of warm cake.

6 Broil about 4 inches from heat 1 to 2 minutes or until topping is bubbly. (Watch closely; topping burns easily.) Cool cake in pan on wire rack. Store tightly covered at room temperature.

Makes 12 servings

Berry Power Drink

1 cup fruit juice (such as orange, cranberry or apple)

1 cup fresh or frozen strawberries

1 container (8 ounces) low-fat vanilla yogurt

⅔ cup **QUAKER® Oats** (quick or old fashioned, uncooked)

1 cup ice cubes

Granulated sugar, to taste

1 Place juice, strawberries, yogurt and oats in blender container. Cover, blend on HIGH speed about 2 minutes or until smooth.

2 Gradually add ice; blend on HIGH speed an additional minute or until smooth. Blend in sugar to taste.

3 Serve immediately.

Makes 2 servings

Quaker's Best Oatmeal Pie

6 egg whites, lightly beaten or ¾ cup egg substitute

⅔ cup firmly packed brown sugar

⅓ cup granulated sugar

¾ cup fat-free milk

1 teaspoon vanilla

1¼ cups **QUAKER® Oats** (quick or old fashioned, uncooked)

¾ cup raisins or other dried fruit such as cherries, cranberries or chopped apricots

½ cup flaked or shredded coconut

½ cup chopped nuts (optional)

1 prepared 9-inch pie crust, unbaked

1 Heat oven to 375°F.

2 Beat egg whites and sugars until well blended. Add milk and vanilla; mix well. Stir in oats, raisins, coconut and nuts; mix well. Pour filling into prepared pie crust.

3 Bake 35 to 45 minutes or until center of pie is set. Cool completely on wire rack. Serve with ice cream or whipped cream. Store, covered, in refrigerator.

Makes 8 servings

Show-Off Desserts & Cobblers

Berry Power Drink

Chocolate Oatmeal Smoothie

1 quart vanilla ice cream
½ cup cold coffee
1 teaspoon hazelnut syrup

¼ cup chocolate syrup
½ cup **QUAKER®** Oats (quick or old fashioned, uncooked)
1½ cups heavy cream

Combine ingredients into blender and blend into a smooth, silk-like consistency. Serve in chilled glasses and enjoy!

Makes 16 servings

Country Oat Cake

CAKE
1 package (18.5 ounces) spice cake mix
1 cup **QUAKER®** Oats (quick or old fashioned, uncooked)
1 cup (8 ounces) low-fat plain yogurt
3 eggs or ¾ cup egg substitute
¼ cup vegetable oil
¼ cup water

1½ cups peeled, finely chopped apples (about 2 medium)

TOPPING
1 cup **QUAKER®** Oats (quick or old fashioned, uncooked)
½ cup firmly packed brown sugar
¼ cup (½ stick) margarine or butter, softened
½ teaspoon ground cinnamon
Whipped cream (optional)

1 Heat oven to 350°F. Grease and flour 13×9-inch baking pan.

2 For cake, combine cake mix, oats, yogurt, eggs, oil and water in large mixing bowl. Blend on low speed of electric mixer until moistened; mix at medium speed for 2 minutes. Stir in apples. Pour into prepared pan. For topping, combine oats, brown sugar, margarine and cinnamon; mix well. Sprinkle evenly over batter.

3 Bake 40 to 45 minutes or until wooden pick inserted in center comes out clean. Serve warm or at room temperature with whipped cream, if desired.

Makes 16 servings

Not-So-Sinful Sundae Pie

CRUST

1 cup **QUAKER® Oats** (quick or old fashioned, uncooked)

½ cup all-purpose flour

5 tablespoons margarine, melted

¼ cup firmly packed brown sugar

FILLING

1 quart fat-free or low-fat vanilla frozen yogurt, softened

2 cups any combination of fresh fruit, such as sliced bananas, blueberries or halved strawberries

Fat-free hot fudge topping or berry-flavored fruit syrup (optional)

1 Heat oven to 350°F. Spray 9-inch pie plate with nonstick cooking spray.

2 Combine oats, flour, margarine and brown sugar in medium bowl; mix well. Press firmly onto bottom and sides of pie plate. Bake 18 to 20 minutes or until golden brown. Cool completely on wire rack.

3 Spoon frozen yogurt into cooled crust, spreading evenly. Cover and freeze until firm, about 5 hours. Remove pie from freezer 10 to 15 minutes before serving. Cut into wedges; top with fruit and fudge sauce, if desired. Store tightly covered in freezer.

Makes 8 servings

Mocha Walnut Crunch Coffeecake

COFFEECAKE

- 1 package (16 ounces) hot roll mix
- 1 cup **QUAKER® Oats** (quick or old fashioned, uncooked)
- ¼ teaspoon salt (optional)
- ¾ cup milk
- ½ cup (1 stick) margarine or butter
- ½ cup granulated sugar
- 3 eggs, room temperature
- ½ cup semisweet chocolate chips

TOPPING

- ½ cup all-purpose flour
- ½ cup granulated sugar
- ¼ cup **QUAKER® Oats** (quick or old fashioned, uncooked)
- 1 tablespoon instant coffee granules or espresso powder
- ½ cup (1 stick) margarine or butter, chilled
- ½ cup semisweet chocolate chips
- ½ cup chopped walnuts

1 Grease 10-inch tube pan or 12-cup bundt pan. For coffeecake, in large mixing bowl, combine hot roll mix (including yeast packet), oats and salt; mix well. In small saucepan, heat milk and margarine over low heat until margarine is melted; remove from heat. Stir in sugar; cool mixture to 120° to 130°F. Add to oat mixture; add eggs. Beat at low speed of electric mixer until well blended. Stir in chocolate chips. Spoon into prepared pan.

2 For topping, combine flour, sugar, oats and coffee granules; cut in margarine with pastry blender or two knives until mixture is crumbly. Stir in chocolate chips and nuts. Sprinkle evenly over top of dough. Cover loosely with plastic wrap. Let rise in warm place 30 to 40 minutes or until nearly doubled in size.

3 Heat oven to 350°F. Bake, uncovered, 45 to 50 minutes or until wooden pick inserted near center comes out clean. Cool in pan 10 minutes. Remove from pan, topping side up, onto wire rack. Cool completely. Store tightly covered.

Makes 16 servings

Note: If hot roll mix is not available, combine 3 cups all-purpose flour, two ¼-ounce packages quick-rising yeast and 1½ teaspoons salt; mix well. Continue as recipe directs.

Easy Apple-Berry Crumble Pie

1½ cups **QUAKER® Oats** (quick or old fashioned, uncooked)

1 cup all-purpose flour

½ cup firmly packed brown sugar

½ teaspoon baking soda

10 tablespoons butter or margarine, melted

1 can (21 ounces) apple pie filling

¾ cup dried cranberries

1½ teaspoons lemon juice

½ teaspoon ground cinnamon

1 Heat oven to 375°F. Lightly spray 8- or 9-inch glass pie plate with nonstick cooking spray.

2 Combine oats, flour, brown sugar and baking soda in medium bowl. Add melted butter; mix well. Set aside ¾ cup oat mixture for topping. Press remaining oat mixture firmly onto bottom and sides of pie plate. Bake 10 to 12 minutes or until light golden brown. Cool slightly on wire rack.

3 Stir together pie filling, cranberries, lemon juice and cinnamon in same bowl. Spoon filling over hot crust, spreading evenly. Sprinkle reserved oat mixture evenly over filling. Bake 18 to 22 minutes or until topping is golden brown. Serve warm or at room temperature.

Makes 8 servings

Apple Spice Cake

TOPPING

- 1 cup **QUAKER® Oats** (quick or old fashioned, uncooked)
- ½ cup firmly packed brown sugar
- ½ teaspoon ground cinnamon
- ¼ cup (½ stick) butter, softened
  Whipped cream (optional)

CAKE

- 1 package (18.5 ounces) spice cake mix
- 1 cup **QUAKER® Oats** (quick or old fashioned, uncooked)
- 1 cup (8 ounces) low-fat plain yogurt
- 3 eggs
- ¼ cup vegetable oil
- ¼ cup water
- 1½ cups finely chopped apples (about 2 medium)

1 Heat oven to 350°F. Spray 13×9-inch metal baking pan with nonstick cooking spray.

2 For topping, combine oats, brown sugar and cinnamon in medium bowl. Cut in butter with 2 knives until mixture is crumbly. Set aside.

3 For cake, combine cake mix, oats, yogurt, eggs, oil and water in large bowl. Blend with electric mixer at low speed until moistened; mix at medium speed 2 minutes. Stir in apples. Pour into pan. Sprinkle topping evenly over batter.

4 Bake 40 to 45 minutes or until wooden pick inserted in center comes out clean. Serve warm or at room temperature with whipped cream, if desired.

Makes 16 servings

Quick Almond Oat Danish Coffee Cake

1 cup plus 2 tablespoons **QUAKER® Oats** (quick or old fashioned, uncooked), divided

5 tablespoons margarine or butter, melted

⅓ cup finely chopped almonds

⅓ cup granulated sugar

2 tablespoons egg substitute or 1 egg white, lightly beaten, divided

¾ teaspoon almond extract

1 pound frozen bread dough, thawed, at room temperature

1 cup whole pitted prunes or mixed dried fruit

1 Spray cookie sheet with nonstick cooking spray or oil lightly.

2 Combine 1 cup oats and margarine in medium bowl; mix well. Stir in almonds, sugar, 1 tablespoon egg substitute and almond extract.

3 Turn bread dough out onto lightly floured surface. Roll or pat dough into 12×10-inch rectangle. Spread oat mixture in narrow strip down middle; top with prunes. On each side of filling, cut 3-inch diagonal slits 2 inches apart. Fold alternating strips of dough over filling to form a braid pattern, pinching ends of strips to seal. Transfer to prepared cookie sheet. Cover; let rise in warm place 30 minutes or until almost doubled in size.

4 Heat oven to 350°F. Brush loaf with remaining 1 tablespoon egg substitute; sprinkle with remaining 2 tablespoons oats.

5 Bake 30 to 35 minutes or until golden brown. Serve warm.

Makes 8 servings

Index

Entrées

Muffins & Scones

Oatmeal

Metric Conversion Chart

VOLUME MEASUREMENTS (dry)

$^1/_8$ teaspoon = 0.5 mL
$^1/_4$ teaspoon = 1 mL
$^1/_2$ teaspoon = 2 mL
$^3/_4$ teaspoon = 4 mL
1 teaspoon = 5 mL
1 tablespoon = 15 mL
2 tablespoons = 30 mL
$^1/_4$ cup = 60 mL
$^1/_3$ cup = 75 mL
$^1/_2$ cup = 125 mL
$^2/_3$ cup = 150 mL
$^3/_4$ cup = 175 mL
1 cup = 250 mL
2 cups = 1 pint = 500 mL
3 cups = 750 mL
4 cups = 1 quart = 1 L

VOLUME MEASUREMENTS (fluid)

1 fluid ounce (2 tablespoons) = 30 mL
4 fluid ounces ($^1/_2$ cup) = 125 mL
8 fluid ounces (1 cup) = 250 mL
12 fluid ounces (1$^1/_2$ cups) = 375 mL
16 fluid ounces (2 cups) = 500 mL

WEIGHTS (mass)

$^1/_2$ ounce = 15 g
1 ounce = 30 g
3 ounces = 90 g
4 ounces = 120 g
8 ounces = 225 g
10 ounces = 285 g
12 ounces = 360 g
16 ounces = 1 pound = 450 g

DIMENSIONS

$^1/_{16}$ inch = 2 mm
$^1/_8$ inch = 3 mm
$^1/_4$ inch = 6 mm
$^1/_2$ inch = 1.5 cm
$^3/_4$ inch = 2 cm
1 inch = 2.5 cm

OVEN TEMPERATURES

250°F = 120°C
275°F = 140°C
300°F = 150°C
325°F = 160°C
350°F = 180°C
375°F = 190°C
400°F = 200°C
425°F = 220°C
450°F = 230°C

BAKING PAN SIZES

Utensil	Size in Inches/Quarts	Metric Volume	Size in Centimeters
Baking or Cake Pan (square or rectangular)	8×8×2	2 L	20×20×5
	9×9×2	2.5 L	23×23×5
	12×8×2	3 L	30×20×5
	13×9×2	3.5 L	33×23×5
Loaf Pan	8×4×3	1.5 L	20×10×7
	9×5×3	2 L	23×13×7
Round Layer Cake Pan	8×1½	1.2 L	20×4
	9×1½	1.5 L	23×4
Pie Plate	8×1¼	750 mL	20×3
	9×1¼	1 L	23×3
Baking Dish or Casserole	1 quart	1 L	—
	1½ quarts	1.5 L	—
	2 quarts	2 L	—